THE

ANATOMY

OF

PREACHING

Also by David L. Larsen

*The Company of the Preachers: A History of Biblical Preaching
from the Old Testament to the Modern Era*

*The Company of the Creative: A Christian Reader's Guide to
Great Literature and Its Themes*

THE
ANATOMY
OF
PREACHING

Identifying the Issues in
Preaching Today

David L. Larsen

kregel
PUBLICATIONS

Grand Rapids, MI 49501

*The Anatomy of Preaching: Identifying the Issues
in Preaching Today*

Copyright © 1989 by David L. Larsen

Published in 1999 by Kregel Publications, a division of Kregel,
Inc., P.O. Box 2607, Grand Rapids, MI 49501. Kregel Publications provides trusted, biblical publications for Christian
growth and service. Your comments and suggestions are val-
ued.

For more information about Kregel Publications, visit our
web site at: www.kregel.com

Cover design: Nicholas G. Richardson

Library of Congress Cataloging-in-Publication Data
Larsen, David L.
    The anatomy of preaching: identifying the issues in
preaching today / David L. Larsen.
        p.   cm.
Originally published: Grand Rapids, Mich.: Baker Book
House, © 1989.
Includes bibliographical references and indexes.
    1. Preaching. I. Title.
BV4211.2.L37   1999   251—dc21   99-24710
                                                    CIP

ISBN 0-8254-3098-4

Printed in the United States of America

1 2 3 4 5 / 03 02 01 00 99

To
my parents,
who have loved so deeply,
listened so frequently,
and prayed so faithfully

Contents

Preface

The current resurgence of interest in preaching comes at a time of cultural transition. While the obituaries which frequently depict the irrelevance and impotence of this craft are premature, there is widespread, justifiable concern for this form of communication in our rapidly changing and increasingly visual society. P. T. Forsyth's dictum stands: "The church rises and falls by preaching." Young preachers and veterans of the pulpit alike need a sharply focused awareness of the key issues facing the pulpit today.

The issues are not difficult to discern. Those discussed in this book have arisen often during my many years of preaching and teaching of homiletics. Certain questions are asked repeatedly at preachers' conferences. The torrent of current literature in the field helps shape our understanding of its frontiers. Thoughtful laypeople inquire as to where the discussions about preaching are taking the church today.

Each of the following fifteen chapters seeks to identify a pressing current issue and to chart a reasonable and prudent course for preachers today. What Frederick W. Robertson termed "the intense excitement of preaching" can be fueled only by thoughtful reflection on the craft.

The intent of this book is not to instruct in the basic art of pulpit communication but to add to that reflection.

To the administration, my faculty colleagues, and students at Trinity Evangelical Divinity School in Deerfield, Illinois, I give grateful acknowledgment for the inestimable debt I owe them; and to my wife, Jean, an ever-deepening appreciation for her buoyant encouragement and unflagging assistance. *Ad gloriam Dei.*

1

Does Preaching Have a Future?
The Issue of Viability

Is preaching on the way out, a casualty of an age which prefers the nonverbal? What are the prospects for preaching in the current communications revolution? Are preachers going to be the hapless victims of their own verbicide?

These are questions which increasingly confront practitioners of the craft. The parish preacher makes an incredible investment of time and effort in several weekly preparations, thousands of sermons over a lifetime, and millions of words. While the preacher is not simply a vendor of words, the three hundred thousand preachers in America are responsible for a massive output. Critics charge that all this effort is a waste of human resources, that the day when the church is stirred by the eloquence of its leaders has passed.

Of course the cultured (and uncultured) despisers of preaching are by no means new to the scene. There have always been dire predictions of the demise of this ancient art, popular disparagement, and cynicism. *Webster's Third International Dictionary* gives as one definition of preaching: "Exhorting in an officious and tiresome manner." Such a definition is reflected in popular culture, as Madonna sings, "Papa, don't preach." Even churchgoers echo the secular disdain to say, "Now, don't start preaching to me!" The negative connotation of the term is clear and painfully cutting.

Every preacher has discouraging moments when the whole enterprise seems futile and precarious. Some sermons come rushing and surging in the study, like molten lava flowing from a Vesuvius. Other messages cause indescribable difficulty. A few have been for me as close to childbirth as I shall ever come. And what burns and lives in preparation does not always ignite in the pulpit. On the brighter side, what seemed stillborn in preparation may resuscitate in delivery. Whatever the individual result, we are called today to defend the viability of all our collective labor. The questions we must answer have become inevitable: Is preaching petering out in our television age? What is the prognosis for preaching in the modern world? What kind of base and foundation does the practice of preaching have in the church of Jesus Christ? Is that base still a strong enough foundation on which to build its future?

The Family Tree of the Sermon

The sermon has been a central institution in the church from its inception and a unique genre in world religious expression, although Judaism and Islam have kindred equivalents. In Buddhism, to be sure, the monks may teach, but that teaching bears no similarity to the formal discourse we call the sermon. In Islam, each Friday, instead of the customary daily prayers, additional recitations of the Koran are given, and the imam or prayer leader shares a *khutbah* or sermon during which he frequently discusses current issues through the elaboration of the sacred text. The imam stands in front of and above the faithful—often inciting and arousing their passions. It is not difficult to see the roots of Islam in Judaism and Christianity.

The sermon is no historical accident. Although culturally shaped as to its form, the sermon, we will argue, has been given by God for the instruction and inspiration of his people and for the propagation of the gospel to the ends of the earth. "And at his appointed season he brought his word to light through the preaching entrusted to me by the command of God our Savior" (Titus 1:3). Thus we may not view the sermon as a fortuitous incidental development. It is part of God's order; hence its remarkable and extraordinary longevity. Humanly speaking, the sermon has no future. It should long since have been relegated to the slag heap of human obsolescence.

The real origin of preaching is to be found in God himself and in his nature. He is addressed as a "God of truth" (Ps. 31:5) and as "a God who knows" (1 Sam. 2:3). The Scriptures describe humankind as created in God's image and, like God, possessing rational, thinking egos. Christ as *Logos* lights every person who comes into the world (John 1:9). God is not silent but has spoken to his human creatures (Heb. 1:1–3). In this we are like him in that we speak to him and to one another. Words and language have thought content, notwithstanding the distortions of meaning caused by sin. The possibility and plausibility of preaching are predicated on the same premise as is all human discourse: God has made us to think and hear and speak.

The Old Testament Roots

The Old Testament pedigree of preaching shows it to be one of the striking continuities between the Old Testament and the New. While there are no formal discourses early on, certainly nothing stylized, spiritual discourses abound. The New Testament speaks of

"Enoch, the seventh from Adam, who prophesied" (Jude 14). Noah is characterized as "a preacher of righteousness" (2 Pet. 2:6). We possess none of the words he spoke during the long years of the preparation of the ark, but we readily assume there was oral communication as well as the symbolic witness of his labors. The valedictory address of Moses, known to us as the Book of Deuteronomy, is really homiletical in form. That means, in the literal roots of the word *homily*, that it says "the same thing as" the Word of God. These perorations invite careful scrutiny since they are ancestral to Christian proclamation. The two farewells of Joshua, found in Joshua 23–24, have similar relevance, as does David's eloquence in worship and praise to God and Solomon's words on the occasion of the dedication of the temple (1 Kings 8). This ancient communication must be viewed as important roots in the family tree of preaching.

In the flowering of the prophets we find the most significant precursors of the glorious company of the preachers. We must conclude that the prophets were preachers. Some of the prophets came from "the schools of the prophets"; others, among them roughhewn Elijah and rugged Amos, knew no such gentility.

Ezra, as both a prophet and a priest, exemplifies rudimentary principle and practice. Ezra was "a teacher well versed in the Law of Moses, which the LORD, the God of Israel, had given" (Ezra 7:6). He "devoted himself to the study and observance of the Law of the LORD, and to teaching its decrees and laws in Israel" (Ezra 7:10). How Ezra read the Book of the Law aloud to the people from daybreak until noon and how they listened attentively to the Book of the Law is movingly chronicled in Nehemiah 8. We see Ezra opening the book, the people standing up in reverence, and Ezra leading them in praises. Then the Levites join him in "making it clear and giving the meaning so that the people could understand what was being read" (Neh. 8:8). The result was great joy as day after day the Word was shared with the assembly.

Preachers today stand in this awesome succession. We are the descendants of these incendiary spokesmen for God in all of their variety and diversity. How different an Isaiah was from a Jeremiah or Ezekiel. We feel we know Hosea and Jonah, but little of the persona of Joel or Nahum comes through. The mystical Zechariah contrasts with the pastoral and hortatory Malachi, the intellectual Habakkuk with the rustic Micah. Yet each in his appointed milieu bore the burden of "Thus saith the Lord!"

The intertestamental development of the synagogue added to the foundation for Christian worship and communication. Yngve T. Brilioth rightly contends that it is "in the synagogue service that the Jewish sermon assumes its form."[1] Here the reading of the Scripture in Hebrew and translation into the vernacular with an explanatory exposition interwove liturgical and exegetical elements in the worship service of the Jews, both in Palestine and in the diaspora. The Jewish targums, with their translations and explanations of Scripture in Aramaic, and the hortatory and applicatory writings known as the *haggadah* are part of our preaching tradition. Our legacy is that of the "Teacher," of whom it was said: "Not only was the Teacher wise, but also he imparted knowledge to the people. He pondered and searched out and set in order many proverbs. The Teacher searched to find just the right words, and what he wrote was upright and true" (Eccles. 12:9–10).

The New Testament Mantle

John the Baptist, "sent from God" as the herald, is the forebear of every gospel preacher. "He himself was not the light; he came only as a witness to the light" (John 1:8). He bridges the Old and New Testaments. His vigorous proclamation moves relentlessly toward a search-

1. Yngve T. Brilioth, *A Brief History of Preaching* (Philadelphia: Fortress, 1965), 4–8.

ing appeal for a verdict. Proclamation and appeal for a
verdict are inseparably conjoined in authentic preaching.
The very vocabulary of preaching in the New Testament
is anchored in the herald's urgency.

"Jesus began to preach" (Matt. 4:17, 23). God's only-
begotten Son was a preacher who rose in the synagogue
in Nazareth to read the Scripture and then, according to
custom, sat to give an authoritative interpretation and
application (Luke 4:16–21). Here is the fountainhead for
all Christian preaching. Preaching is not our invention
for representing God but an essential implication of his
mighty deeds and revelation to us. Christ's works and
words are bound together as the gospel. While we probably do not possess the whole of any single discourse of
our Lord we have portions of at least forty-eight messages and can analyze the approach and method of the
Master-teacher. "Preach the good news to all creation"
(Mark 16:15) comes as the marching orders of the living
Christ, and it is to this mandate that we seek to be faithful in our own time.

The primacy of preaching in the early church does not
come, then, as a surprise, even when the tone is set by
Peter, now not cowering but rather courageous, standing
up on Pentecost. He is saturated with and skilled in the
Scripture (Acts 2:14–40), both because he has learned in
the classroom of the Master-teacher and because he has
been filled with the Spirit of God. These are perennial
hallmarks of the genuine gospel preacher. He keys his
message carefully to his audience, his aim is clear (Acts
2:36), he uses a definite arrangement in his argument,
and he moves aggressively to his conclusion and application. It is salutary for us to consider such a divinely
inspired prototypical preacher and his experience.

Stephen, coming out of Hellenistic culture, is a different kind of preacher. His argument in Acts 7 is similar
to that of the Epistle to the Hebrews. The fearless force-

fulness of his preaching has blazed the trail for those who would not be hirelings who flee or men-pleasers who fawn.

The preaching of the apostle Paul is powerful from the start:[2] "At once he began to preach in the synagogue that Jesus is the Son of God" (Acts 9:20). The Book of Acts shows the apostle preaching in divergent settings. In Antioch of Pisidia, speaking largely to Jews of the dispersion (Acts 13:16–41), the elevation in his preaching focuses on the Lord Jesus Christ and his resurrection. In Athens Paul demonstrates adaptation to audience, using an orderly and logical argument to lead his hearers from where they are to a call to repentance and accountability in the light of Christ's resurrection (Acts 17:16–34). Only one sermon of Paul recorded in Acts is directed to believers (Acts 20:17–38).

It would seem clear that in the New Testament can be found our message and our method. Equally certain is that preaching is a divinely ordained vehicle for the promulgation of the Good News. This fact does not rule out other means, but it does assure us that in all ages of church history preaching will remain a valid central form of communication. Paul speaks of his eagerness to preach in Romans 1:15 and unabashedly observes that "God was pleased through the foolishness of what was preached to save those who believe" (1 Cor. 1:21). "Although I am less than the least of all God's people, this grace was given me: to preach to the Gentiles the unsearchable riches of Christ," he declares in Ephesians 3:8. This is the mantle which falls no less on the preacher sixty generations later, as well as the cry, "Woe to me if I preach not the gospel!" (1 Cor. 9:16).

---

2. John Eadie, *Paul the Preacher; or, A Popular and Practical Exposition of His Discourses and Speeches, as Recorded in the Acts of the Apostles* (London: Richard Griffin and Co., 1959).

The Preachers of Power in
Church History

The Early Church Fathers

The fusion of this rich Old and New Testament heredity has given birth to a spiritual organism, the church, of which Christ is the head. Like her preaching, the church is often flawed, but she is Christ's church and "the gates of Hades will not overcome [her]" (Matt. 16:18). The history of the church underscores how perilous and harrowing have been the risks of preaching through the ages. The venerable craft has lasted despite great opposition and many vicissitudes.

Innumerable preachers in the early centuries built on the prophets and apostles, but none more luminously than John of Antioch, Chrysostom (A.D. c. 343–407). He is recognized as the greatest preacher in the early centuries after the apostles, and his one thousand extant sermons are an exegetical treasury. His use of Scripture was in the Antiochian tradition of exegesis. This means he was obsessed to find the literal and historical meaning of the text, and he demonstrates the somewhat overwrought style of his age. Chrysostom's power may be understood partly in the joy by which he exclaimed, "Preaching makes me well; as soon as I open my mouth to speak, my weariness is forgotten."[3]

The late fourth and early fifth centuries, the age of Chrysostom, Ambrose, and Augustine, was a great time of preaching before seven centuries of decline. Augustine was the greatest Latin preacher. His 360 extant sermons and early work on the art of preaching, *De Doctrina Christiana,* show us the continuing challenge of contextualization in preaching. Since he was addressing the Greco-Roman world, Augustine used Aristotle's *Rhetoric,*

---

3. John Chrysostom, *Homilies of St. John Chrysostom on the Gospel of St. Matthew,* trans. Reverend Sir George Prevost (Grand Rapids: Eerdmans, 1956), 88:523.

Cicero, and the classical frame of reference as the molding and shaping form for the transmission of the Word. In homiletics, as in theology proper, contextualization is necessary but hazardous. In every age, our own not excepted, communicators must take into rigorous account the thought categories and configurations of the hearers. We must exegete culture as well as Scripture if we are to faithfully and authentically communicate the Word. Much more will be said about this later.

The Reformers

The Reformation involved a great revival of preaching. The pulpit was to be higher than the altar. Martin Luther (1483–1546) has left us twenty-three hundred sermons out of his prodigious preaching and writing output. Luther saw preaching as an eschatological struggle in which "Christ is always to be preached." The text was to control the sermon and was to be aimed at the heart as well as the mind. His preaching was filled with pictures and could be described as "heroic disorder." For John Calvin (1509–1564), preaching was also central. His one thousand extant sermons show this gifted preacher going book by book through Scripture to help his people achieve a sense of the connectedness of the Word. He never soared rhetorically and was without strength in metaphor, imagery, or imagination. He maintained that "God has ordained His Word as the instrument by which Jesus Christ, with all His graces, is dispensed to us." Theodore Beza said of his preaching, "Every word weighs a pound."[4] Ulrich Zwingli (1884–1531) led the Reformation movement in Zurich and did not write out his sermons. The awakening came to Zurich as Zwingli began to preach through the Gospel of Matthew. His voice was weak and his delivery rapid, but his preaching

4. T. Harwood Pattison, "Theodore Beza," *The History of Christian Preaching* (Philadelphia: American Baptist Publication Society, 1903), 144.

aimed at producing a changed heart and had a definite
and practical turn.

The history of preaching presents a notable succession
of preachers in incredibly contrasting situations and cir-
cumstances, in all cultures and in the face of great
controversy and spiritual conflict. There have been ebbs
and flows, but God has continued to own and bless
the preaching of his Word. God's commendation of the
Word preached is evident in the power of John Knox,
John Donne, John Wesley, George Whitefield, Jonathan Edwards, Charles Haddon Spurgeon, Alexander
Maclaren, John Henry Jowett, Joseph Parker, G. Campbell Morgan, and in others to the present hour. Indeed
it is undeniable that where preaching thrives, the church
thrives. Any factor analysis of spiritual health and vitality among the people of God does not fail to show the
importance of preaching in the equation. Strong biblical
preaching correlates closely with a spiritually effective
ministry and witness.

Case Study of Impact

A striking instance is described by Dr. Harry S. Stout
of Yale University in his recent definitive treatment of
preaching in colonial New England, *The New England
Soul.*[5] Stout relates that the New England sermon of the
seventeenth and eighteenth centuries was a medium of
communications "whose topical range and social influence were so powerful in shaping cultural values, meanings and a sense of corporate purpose that even television
pales in comparison."[6] Stout argues that the impact of
these more than five million messages across the colonial
period was decisive. The average New Englander heard
seven thousand sermons in a lifetime, amounting to

5. Harry S. Stout, *The New England Soul* (New York: Oxford University
Press, 1986).
6. Ibid., 3.

approximately fifteen thousand hours of concentrated listening.

The people in New England were "a unique 'people of the Word.'" As Stout points out, "The meetinghouse's position at the center of the community also signified submission to God's power, the power that came to a people who subordinated all human authorities and institutions to the infallible rule of *Sola Scriptura*."[7] Preaching molded the families and communities of New England. The preached Word under the Holy Spirit became foundational for the values and ideals of this seminal society. To quote Stout again: "The ministers enjoyed awesome powers in New England society. . . . [Y]et, because sermons had to be based on *Sola Scriptura*, even the ministers' authority was limited."[8] And what was the basic reality in New England has been, is now, and will be the fact until Jesus comes again.

There are many gnawing issues for the Christian communicator nearing the end of the twentieth century. There is much work to be done in what is a gargantuan task for the preacher in this age as in all other ages. But we may be confident of the viability of true biblical preaching, wherever or whenever we may be. Preach the Word!

7. Ibid., 14.
8. Ibid., 19.

2

What Is Biblical Preaching?
The Issue of Authority

What is the Word of God and why is it to be preached? Before we can discuss how to preach the Word of God we must grapple with the nature of the Word and its authority. It is not at all clear to many who preach, nor to our culture as a whole, that a preacher should be *The Servant of the Word,* to use Herbert H. Farmer's apt book title.[1]

Authority is one of the most crucial and controversial questions of our time. Bernard L. Ramm has stated the crux of the issue in his definition of authority as "that right or power to command action or compliance, or to determine belief or custom, expecting obedience from those under authority, and in turn giving responsible account for the claim to right or power."[2]

Modern men and women revolt against traditional and received authorities. The whole notion of obedience to commands and authority has always been difficult for

1. Herbert H. Farmer, *The Servant of the Word* (New York: Charles Scribner's Sons, 1942).
2. Bernard L. Ramm, *The Pattern of Religious Authority* (Grand Rapids: Eerdmans, 1957), 10.

22

fallen humankind, but in the egalitarian climate of today's world the idea is absurd to many. We aspire to be autonomous beings, subject to no higher rule than self-inclination. The contemporary rebellion against authority can be seen in the arenas of government, education, the home, and the church. This has implications for the preacher.

Carl F. H. Henry rightly observes, "Nowhere does the crisis of modern theology find a more critical center than in the controversy over the reality and nature of divine disclosure."[3] Some go so far as to question whether there is objective truth and whether truth, if it exists, can be known. So strong is the aversion to the objectivity of revealed truth in some circles that there is virtually a total withdrawal to nonrational categories.

The historic faith of the Christian church is clear in these matters, holding that the Bible is the only infallible guide to faith, doctrine, and practice. Emil Brunner noted that the fate of the Bible is the fate of Christianity. The principle of the Reformation was *Sola Scriptura.* Our authority is the Bible. Ramm is correct in asserting, "The Holy Spirit speaking in the Scriptures, which are the product of the Spirit's revelatory and inspiring action, is the principle of authority for the Christian Church."[4]

"Has God Said?"

The widespread effective loss of the authority of the Bible in Christendom has had a lamentable effect on preaching generally, echoing God's question to Jeremiah, "Since they have rejected the word of the LORD, what kind of wisdom do they have?" (Jer. 8:9b). The full authority of the Bible was unquestioned within the

3. Carl F. H. Henry, *God, Revelation and Authority,* vol. 2 (Waco: Word, 1976), 7.

4. Ramm, *The Pattern of Religious Authority,* 28.

church for centuries. What we see today is a tragic breach in the Reformation principle, erosion of confidence in the authority of Scripture that looks to the human-centered "enlightenment" instead of the God-centered Reformation.

This whittling away of our heritage has left some preachers holding a Bible which is for them only a human record of man's response to God. Hendrik W. Van Loon spoke of the Old Testament as a national Jewish scrapbook, a kind of *Reader's Digest* anthology. Such a Bible is no longer communication; it is only communion. To those who find miraculous and supernatural revelation repugnant, the revelation vouchsafed to Moses at Sinai is no different from the one claimed by the Gnostic writer who received the gospel of Poimandres or that given to Arjuna who received a theophany of the god Krishna. Even David Strauss, a notorious skeptic, described this view as the disintegration of "the orthodox doctrine of Scripture."

The attempt to build some authority base for proclamation on the natural data of the physical universe or human conscience or religious experience effectively leaves us without authority. The scissors-and-paste approach also removes the Bible from laypeople . . . only the Ph.D. seems capable of sorting truth from error. J. I. Packer calls this the paradox of the critical movement: "It has given the Church the Bible in a way that has deprived the Church of the Bible, and led to a famine of hearing the words of the Lord."[5] The rationalistic critic has become a salvage man rather than a careful clarifier of the sacred text.

The effect of the modern demolition of scriptural authority has been catastrophic. Without Scripture as the *principium unicum,* as the Reformers insisted, theology is in chaos. If there is no significant difference

5. J. I. Packer, *God Speaks to Man: Revelation and the Bible* (Philadelphia: Westminster, 1965), 13.

between the Bible and Aesop's *Fables* or Joseph Smith's tablets we are abandoned with a hopeless mixture of truth and error calculated to foster hesitation and equivocation in the pulpit. Deprived of normative consensus as to authoritative content, the preacher turns to pop psychology, current events, or book reviews to feed his famished flock. Packer correctly argues that preaching has been undermined and the church enfeebled by "the loss of the historic conviction that what Scripture says, God says."[6] Truth is essential for trust. If the Bible is a witness is it a false witness? If the Bible is to be judge of error shall we adjudge it to be in error? Where does that leave us?

"Is There Any Word from God?"

"God has spoken!" is the sure premise of all biblical preaching; human language has been employed for divine service. Although language is culturally conditioned and therefore relative, it can express literal truth. I can, with all of my limitations, both write and speak propositions which correspond to reality. Words in Scripture propositionally describe revelatory deeds and interpret these events through the Holy Spirit.

Citing the death of the Lord Jesus Christ as a historical event, George Eldon Ladd notes the need for divine interpretation:

> Paul says that it [the death of Christ] is the proof, the demonstration of the love of God (Rom. 5:8). How do we know that Christ's death discloses the love of God? Were the Roman soldiers conscious of God's love as they watched Jesus die? Were the few disciples who stayed close to the cross drawn there because they realized that in this act God was demonstrating his love for them? . . . Does Golgotha speak for itself? On the contrary, the disciples thought that the end of their world had come. . . .

6. Ibid., 18.

Only when the Resurrection reversed the apparent catastrophe of his death, only when the risen Christ himself interpreted the meaning of his death (Luke 24:26–27), only when the apostles set forth the unseen, divine activity in an otherwise tragic event, did it begin to convey a new significance and to be recognized for what it was: an act of God's love. We know that Jesus' death shows the love of God only because of the prophetic interpretation of that event.[7]

The vagaries of liberal theology, whether Roman Catholic or Protestant, will not yield a "thus saith the Lord" for the preacher. The subjectivism of dialectical theology offers us no foundation on which to build. Television journalist Ted Koppel made a surprisingly eloquent condemnation of subjectivism in a commencement address: "Truth is not a polite tap on the shoulder; it is a howling reproach. What Moses brought down from Mount Sinai were not the Ten Suggestions; they are Commandments. Are, not were. The sheer beauty of the Commandments is that they codify in a handful of words acceptable human behavior, not just for then or now, but for all time."[8] It is this objective relevance of the divinely given Word that braces and buttresses proclamation so that it is more than speculation.

This is why William E. Gladstone, the great British prime minister, spoke of the Bible as "the impregnable rock of Holy Scripture," and Charles Haddon Spurgeon, one of the mightiest of all preachers, described the issue of the authority of the Bible as a decisive battle, "the Thermopylae of the Christian faith." The Lausanne Covenant of 1974 took wise and high ground when it asserted in the face of all of the difficulties, "The Bible is inerrant in all that it affirms." As Edward John Car-

7. George Eldon Ladd, "Revelation, History and the Bible," *Christianity Today* 1 (September 30, 1957): 7.
8. Ted Koppel, *Religion and Society Report* 5, 1 (January 1988), 3.

nell, building on the ideas of Benjamin B. Warfield, perceived so clearly: "We are closed up to the teaching of the Bible for our information about *all* doctrines in the Christian faith, and this includes the doctrine of the Bible's view of itself."[9] In fact the Bible nowhere protests against the identification of Scripture with divine revelation. The writers do not correct each other. The New Testament writers do not question the Old Testament.

Our attitude toward Scripture is important if we are to approach genuinely biblical preaching with confidence in the coherence and the nonself-contradictory nature of the biblical text. The undercutting of such confidence has serious implications for our preaching. Regarding these implications, Donald Grey Barnhouse insightfully critiqued *The Interpreter's Bible,* which is certainly one of the most widely used and foremost sets of biblical interpretation produced in this century. The commentator on Hebrews 4:3–6 finds the biblical writer's argument to be defective, a problem he also identifies in Hebrews 7.[10] Then he says: "The fact that no responsible scholar today would juggle the scripture in this fashion must not be allowed to obscure the underlying thought of the writer."[11] Barnhouse minced no words in condemning this attack on the Holy Spirit. We would add, if the author of Hebrews juggled the Scripture, how shall the preacher faithfully follow the text as written? An element of uncertainty and dubiety has crept into the manner in which Scripture is to be regarded and reverenced and this has immense ramification for preaching it.

---

9. Edward John Carnell, letter to the editor, *Christianity Today* 23 (October 14, 1966): 23.

10. Alexander C. Purdy, exegesis, "The Epistle to the Hebrews," *The Interpreter's Bible,* ed. George A. Buttrick, 12 vols. (Nashville: Abingdon, 1955), 11:630–31, 660–66.

11. Donald Grey Barnhouse, "Always It Is God Speaking," *Eternity* 11 (November 1960): 26–27.

"The Word of the Lord Is
Offensive to Them"

The practical fallout of our position on biblical authority for our preaching can be clearly seen in David G.
Buttrick's recent volume, *Homiletic*.[12] This is an extraordinary, seminal work which has lasting implications.
Buttrick's avowed goal is to go back to square one in the
crafting of preaching and "to understand what may
actually take place in consciousness during the produc-
tion and hearing of sermons."[13] Abandoning many of the
hoary and time-honored foundations of classical rhetoric
and homiletical theory, he exegetes culture with consum-
mate skill and breaks new ground in areas we shall have
occasion to observe subsequently. Buttrick gives a brilliant critique of the inadequacy of the therapeutic model
of Harry Emerson Fosdick and the human potential
movement. He makes a strong case against pietism, deci-
sionism, conversionism, personalism, and fundamental-
ism. He distances himself sharply from the "salvation
history" movement and the conception of sermons as
recital and therefore from Karl Barth's notion of the sermon as the last link in the chain of revelation.

But he leaves the preacher no better off in the end. We
have at our disposal "the symbols of revelation" but no
real revelation at all behind the symbols. There is no
commanding sense of a divine given. "Human understandings are what we have. . . . There is no certifiable
Christian faith for us to embrace."[14] We draw upon Scripture only secondarily. "Why must every sermon feature
scriptural citation?" he inquires.[15] This is not the question of a biblical preacher.

The bankruptcy of this position with respect to pulpit

12. David G. Buttrick, *Homiletic: Moves and Structures* (Philadelphia: Fortress, 1987).
13. Ibid., xii.
14. Ibid., 408.
15. Ibid., 418.

authority is appallingly apparent. Buttrick teaches that the resurrection narrative of Mark 16:1–8 has meaning "on a symbolic level"; such stories may not be preached in a here-is-what-actually-happened historical style. While the resurrection was surely an event, stories of a risen Christ speak to faith symbolically; they do not give us actual descriptions of the risen Christ or of the sensory experience of witnesses.[16] We are told that we are not dealing with objective history in relation to the resurrection and we must try to "distance a congregation from questions of historicity."[17] The preacher need not, in Buttrick's view, "expound texts slavishly week by week. . . . What is essential in scripture is the story of God-with-us, and not discrete texts basking in their own inerrancy."[18] The locus of authority on this sea of subjectivity is ostensibly *Solus Christus*! But without the indefectible authority of Scripture we must inquire: Which Christ?

Buttrick insists that we do not preach from a text but from within a field of consciousness. The test of this approach is his use of models and illustrative examples. How shall we face the question of the ordination of a homosexual? The preferred answer is that "Of course, if sinlessness is a requirement for ordination, we shall have no clergy. Besides, does homosexuality interfere with a minister's true work, namely preaching and conducting sacraments? According to the Gospel we are all sinners and we are all forgiven in the Cross."[19] This would have been a good place to reach for the Bible for some light from God to shed upon the subject and share with the people.

It is clear that what we believe about the Bible will determine how we shall approach the preaching of the Bible. If we do not believe that the Bible is divinely given

16. Ibid., 400.
17. Ibid., 403.
18. Ibid., 232.
19. Ibid., 429.

revelation from God, miraculous and supernatural, we shall see it as a smorgasbord from which to pick and choose. But if we believe the Bible is truly the Word of God, then we must seek to preach "the whole counsel of God" as reliably set forth on its pages.

"Preach the Word . . ."

Biblical preaching, then, is confident, Spirit-empowered proclamation and application of what the Bible teaches. This proclamation needs to be balanced and proportionate. One might proclaim an aspect of biblical truth to the exclusion of other related and vital truths which are also taught in Scripture and so be utterly unbiblical in the proclamation. We must not build a temple where Scripture erects only a tent. Biblical preaching is proclaiming what the Bible teaches, rightly and reverently. To discern what is right and reverent requires the conscientious commitment of the preacher to wrestle with both the meaning and the significance of the text. The imposition of our own ideas can dilute and distort the biblical message. To preach biblically is an awesome responsibility.

Several years ago at a Bible camp in northern Minnesota, I watched beautiful little hummingbirds drinking a special solution from a feeder. They hovered and whirred about in fascinating maneuvers. The kind folk who fed these creatures advised me that great care must be taken to be sure the solution is not too weak, for then the hummingbirds would be weakened and perhaps unable to fly to their distant destinations in seasonal migration. Similar concern must be taken that preaching be richly biblical and faithful to the intent of the human and divine authors. Too thin a solution can cause a debilitating deprivation. There are several classic kinds of sermons, each of which may be biblical and any one of which can be in a given instance altogether unbiblical:

The homily is a brief series of observations and exhortations based on a short passage of Scripture. It is commonly used at funerals, weddings, and other special occasions when a longer or more carefully elaborated address would be inappropriate.

The topical sermon brings together what Scripture teaches as a whole on a given subject. Topical preaching has a venerable place in the history of the craft. Its legitimacy is seen in the validity of biblical and systematic theology. While this should not be the first choice of the pastor-teacher, every pastor will preach topically on occasion. To preach on abortion, or divorce and remarriage, or the role of women in ministry, or what the Bible teaches about the healing of the body will most likely be topical in nature. Because the topical sermon can be more relentlessly unitary, one discovers that any list of the ten sermons which have most decisively influenced world culture and society consists mostly if not entirely of topical sermons.

The textual-topical sermon is anchored in a biblical text of such brevity that the development of thought is akin to that of the topical sermon. We may preach a series on the Ten Commandments, or the Beatitudes, or the "fruit of the Spirit," or the articles of "the whole armor of God." If I preach on the first commandment, "You shall have no other gods before me," there is not sufficient in the text itself to shape the form of the sermon. Barnhouse and D. Martyn Lloyd-Jones frequently took a very small piece of text and in a kind of inverted pyramid would bring much of the systematic teaching of Scripture to bear upon that seminal text. This approach can be richly biblical, as it was with these master preachers, or it can be biblically threadbare and disjointed.

The textual sermon consists of a verse or two in which the development of the main points falls right out of the word order in the text. There is something singularly satisfying to the preacher when the text itself dictates the configuration of the sermon. Spurgeon would occasionally preach textually, although the preponderance of his preaching was textual-topical. The more microscopic examination of a small portion of text can provide a welcome change of pace. Whether the portion be long or short, great care must be taken to consider the portion within its context. This is still our challenge even when the text is an entire chapter.

The expository sermon must be the preferred form for the pastor-teacher anxious to feed the flock systematically. *Lectio selecta* or choosing, service by service, what text is to be preached runs a greater risk of imbalance or preaching one's personal predilections than does *lectio continua,* systematically preaching through books of the Bible or using a lectionary of texts following the church year. Expository preaching draws both main points and the subpoints from the natural thought unit of the text. This is biblicality at its very best and models for the congregation the way the Word of God is to be handled and studied as does no other kind of preaching. The historic weakness in expository preaching is its common lack of unity. It becomes a kind of didactic running commentary on the text, a cluster of sermonettes. Any sermon needs to basically say one thing just as each of Paul's sermons in Acts centers around a single, unifying thought. The effective expositor revels in the infinite richness of the enscripturated Word, but resists bypaths and such detail that the auditors are lost. All preaching involves careful selectivity.

Whatever form preaching may take, our charge and challenge are to preach biblically because of what we believe about the Bible. Various cultures value different forms of discourse as, for example, in the African church or in the black church in the United States. In all cases the call is for biblical preaching.

"The Word of God Is Living and Active"

God has promised to bless his Word in the salvation of the lost, the upbuilding and maturing of believers, and the edification and stimulation of the church. The power of God's Word is seen in creation; celebrated in Hebrew poetry such as Psalm 119, "the Song of the Word," and corroborated in history. The history of the Bible and of biblical preaching is a miracle story.

The Book of Acts describes a supernatural, spiritual explosion which turned the then-known world upside down. The apostles were dedicated to "prayer and the ministry of the word" (Acts 6:4). The result follows: "So the word of God spread. The number of disciples in Jerusalem increased rapidly, and a large number of priests became obedient to the faith" (Acts 6:7). Arrogant human structures were demolished as "the word of God continued to increase and spread" (Acts 12:24). The citadels of idolatry and evil were devastated so that we read that "the word of the Lord spread widely and grew in power" (Acts 19:20). So the story continues to this hour.

One of the greatest needs in the church today is for truly biblical preaching. In the face of the doubts, confusion, and bewilderment of our time, the clarion summons in this critical hour is for preaching which has "no uncertain sound." Billy Graham ought to be our model of commitment to Scripture. In his widely reported testimony, he relates his doubts and uncertainties as a young minister and how he knelt before the Lord with his Bible open, and earnestly prayed: "Lord, many things in this Book I do not understand. But you have said, 'The just shall live by faith.' All I have received from you I have taken by faith. Here and now I accept the Bible as your Word. I take it all. I take it all without reservation. Where there are things I cannot understand, I will reserve judgment until I receive more light. If this pleases you, give me authority as I proclaim your Word and through that authority convict men and women of sin and turn sinners to the Savior."[20]

20. Billy Graham, "Biblical Authority in Evangelism," *Christianity Today* 1, 1 (1956): 5–6.

3

What Is the Climate for Today's Sermonic Communication?

The Issue of Ecology

Communicators through the centuries have walked in the steps of Aristotle and his *Rhetoric*. Perhaps we have been too slavish to his system, and certainly we who preach must reexamine our debits and credits. We need to remember that Aristotle did not invent the law of contradiction. Yet it is not likely that we shall better Aristotle's classic divisions of discourse: *logos*—the message; *ethos*—the speaker; and *pathos*—the audience.

Some Continental thinkers have disparaged audience analysis. In this vein Dietrich Ritschl has correctly insisted that "the proclamation of the will of God does not depend upon the situation and history of the world."[1] The Bible, after all, is a record of facts, and we cannot with integrity bend and shape its data to accommodate the whims and fads of modernity. Thus, while we do not base preaching on audience analysis, there is no preaching without a congregation.

The Lord Jesus analyzed the different kinds of soil,

1. Dietrich Ritschl, *A Theology of Proclamation* (Richmond: John Knox, 1960), 21.

not in order to change the seed but to help us with the riddle of response. The preacher must take into account the audience to be addressed. Many elements in our strategy of contextualizing the Scripture relate with the situation of our hearers. Audience analysis is defined by Wayne Minnick in his *Art of Persuasion* as "the application of all that is known about human behavior in general to a specific audience in order to anticipate or evaluate their response to a particular persuasive communication."[2] Adaptation of approach must be considered during preparation of the sermon, while the sermon is being delivered, and after the presentation. The danger is that there will be a dialogue of the deaf or what Daniel T. Niles lamented when he observed, "We have lost contact with the world."

A more sophisticated and technical approach is seen in the "audience criticism" of J. Arthur Baird, who quotes T. W. Manson as saying that "both as to matter and method the teaching of Jesus is conditioned by the nature of the audience."[3] Ninety-eight percent of the gospel *logia* are identified as to audience. Baird speaks of the four different audiences which Jesus addressed and analyzes the contrasting patterns employed to reach each. The disciples of Jesus, for instance, are characterized by a lack of understanding, a sense of wonder, persistent disbelief, and opposition to Jesus.[4] The words of Jesus are spoken to their condition. Preachers in all ages and situations must emulate their Master in doing the same. What, then, is the climate today for sermonic communication?

"Destroyed from Lack of Knowledge"

Sometimes the preacher feels like one trying to penetrate a turtle shell with a rye straw. Part of what plagues

2. Wayne Minnick, *Art of Persuasion* (Boston: Houghton Mifflin, 1957), 33.
3. J. Arthur Baird, *Audience Criticism and the Historical Jesus* (Philadelphia: Westminster, 1969), 18.
4. Ibid., 36.

our house is a general cultural illiteracy in our society. There is strong evidence of a mounting biblical and theological illiteracy in our more conservative churches.

A staggering estimate of 61 percent of our population cannot benefit from the average high-school textbook. Eric D. Hirsch, Jr., has given us an epochal analysis of the broader problem in his *Cultural Illiteracy.*[5] Grade-school and high-school achievement scores have been steadily falling, and the achievement levels of top students are markedly decreasing. Hirsch sees the growing lack of "basic information needed to thrive in the modern world." He identifies five thousand terms—names, events, dates—which are needed as shared information but are unknown among a growing group in our society. This has immense implication for the gospel communicator.

Pressing home a similar point with reference to higher education, Allan Bloom's *The Closing of the American Mind*[6] traces how the failure of higher education has impoverished the souls of today's students. The book is a powerful indictment of the prevailing relativism in our culture; in it Bloom states unequivocally: "In the United States, practically speaking, the Bible was the only common culture, one that united simple and sophisticated, rich and poor, young and old, and . . . provided access to the seriousness of books."[7] But this common culture is disappearing.

The almost incredible disappearance of the knowledge of the Bible in our time led George Steiner, writing in the *New Yorker,* to mourn: "One is, indeed, tempted to define modernism in Western culture in terms of the recession of the Old and New Testaments from the common currency of recognition. . . . [S]uch recognition was

---

5. Eric D. Hirsch, Jr., *Cultural Illiteracy: What Every American Needs to Know* (New York: Houghton Mifflin, Vintage Books, 1987).

6. Allan Bloom, *The Closing of the American Mind* (New York: Simon and Schuster, 1987).

7. Ibid., 58.

the sinew of literacy, the shared matter of intellect and sentiment from the sixteenth century onward ... the lapse of the Scriptural from the everyday in the commerce of ideas and proposals, of warning and promise in our body politic in the West entails a veritable breakdown of solidarity, of concord within dissent."[8] This tragic loss of the Bible as a point of reference has to be faced by the communicator committed to biblical preaching.

It is amusing to hear of the person who thought libido was the devil and that neurosis and psychosis were two women in the Bible, but it is distressing that increasing ignorance and disuse of the Bible are in evidence among those who profess to believe the Bible. Half of the Protestants polled could list four or fewer of the Ten Commandments. Five hundred million Bibles are in circulation but 40 percent of Protestants read it "never or hardly ever."[9] One study found that 63 percent of church-going Protestants surveyed could not note a difference between Old and New Testaments, few knew a single thing about the prophets, and few could apply the story of the good Samaritan to life. Biblical materials as such were "only slightly comprehended."[10] What is the problem?

"Never Coming to the Knowledge of the Truth"

Whatever the causes, the preacher finds the situation rough going. A young pastor from Arizona writes to me that in his sermons, "I've been discouraged at how little people glean from all that I share. I really preach my heart out and I prepare diligently, but I wonder how

8. "For the Babble Tells Me So," *Context* 20 (March 15, 1988): 3.

9. Martin E. Marty, *Religion and Republic: The American Circumstance* (Boston: Beacon, 1987), 157.

10. Ibid., 159.

much sinks in." The fact is we are living in a communications revolution. As the Dutch philosopher Arend van Leewen argues, we have moved with rapidity and suddenness from the ontocratic era, with its unified sense of cosmic reality, to the technological era which is functional, pragmatic, thoroughly secular.[11]

We can characterize the current situation for communication in our culture by some of its basic components:

Overstimulation. Ours is an information society and a visual society. The average household has the television set on seven hours a day. The average young person in our culture has spent twelve thousand hours in school by the time of high-school graduation and fifteen thousand hours in front of the television set. No previous generation has ever been so overstimulated by an unrelenting barrage of images, sights, and sounds.

Desensitization. This constant media blitz results in a mood of perpetual crisis. We immediately and instantaneously become aware of disasters, crises, and violence through communications satellites. The plausibility of the whole world seeing the two slain witnesses on the streets of Jerusalem (Rev. 11:8–10) is now very striking. The continuous anesthesia of the media builds a defense mechanism against stimuli. In self-defense we discount what we hear and see. We are not able to feel the shock of violence and horror because we have seen so much. We are not moved and upended easily.

Enervation. The average person feels overwhelmed as nations and institutions and persons stagger from crisis to crisis. What can I do about anything? We

11. William F. Fore, "The Church and Communication in the Technological Era," *Christian Century* 103 (September 24, 1986): 810–12.

seem as tiny chips carried on the pounding surf of a great, turbulent sea. Change appears unlikely. Bertrand Russell said that we human beings are like sick flies clinging dizzily to the rapidly turning rotors of a dynamo. We are stunned and stupified in the face of the enormity of the issues facing modern societies.

Depersonalization. In all of this the individual seems to count for less and less. We are merely numbers, ciphers of little consequence. We are fear in a handful of dust. Think of the great message we have to share from the Scripture about a God who genuinely knows and cares, who counts the very number of the hairs on our heads. Yet we address people who feel inconsequential, pulverized, and put down.

Preference for the nonverbal. Words, propositions, and carefully reasoned arguments are less appealing than images, and most preachers tend to be image-poor communicators whose specialty is propositional revelation and who preach best from the didactic sections of Scripture. Ours is an age attuned to feeling, while many of us preach in a context still reacting against excess in feeling.

Confusion. Many are left limp and prostrate in the clatter of conflicting voices. There have always been competitive truth claims in this din of inequity in which we live, but how shall we find our way amid the superhardsell and subliminal messages on every side? We feel buffeted in the crosscurrents of higher criticism, narcissism, existentialism, materialism, and nihilism. Hearers seem numb and inert.

One of the most provocative and probing analyses of what is happening on the contemporary communications scene is Neil Postman's *Amusing Ourselves to Death*. Postman, professor of communications at New York University, argues that Americans have descended into a vast triviality which is causing the dissolution of public discourse. Television is the paradigm: "On television discourse is conducted largely through visual imagery, which is to say that television gives us a conversation in images, not words. The emergence of the image-manager in the political arena and the concomitant decline of the speech-writer attest to the fact that television demands a different kind of content from other media. Its form works against the content."[12]

Postman asserts that our very idea of what truth is has changed as the result of leaving a print culture in which people read. "From its beginning until well into the nineteenth century, America was dominated by the printed word and an oratory based on the printed word . . . this situation was only in part a legacy of the Protestant tradition."[13] The discourses of the great communicators of our history, secular and sacred, were modeled after the printed page in what Postman calls this "Age of Exposition."

The first step toward becoming an image-centered culture was the telegraph, which released "demons of discourse," large-scale irrelevance, impotence, and incoherence. Now decontextualized information causes us to float in an ocean of information, greatly altering what Postman calls the "information-action ratio." Formerly, "what people knew had action-value. . . . Thus we have here a great loop of impotence: the news elicits a variety of opinions about which you can do nothing except to offer them as more news, about which you can do nothing."[14]

Of course, the new world brings benefits—entertainment is fine. But modern television has become our cul-

12. Neil Postman, *Amusing Ourselves to Death: Public Discourse in the Age of Show Business* (New York: Viking, 1985), 7.
13. Ibid., 41.
14. Ibid., 69.

ture, changing our lives into "one vast arena for show business."[15] Television is the metaphor for all discourse. Everything must have entertainment value. The commercial which succeeds is entertaining. The program which holds interest is entertaining. There must be a never-ending succession of new, tantalizing, scintillating images. "As typography once dictated the style of conducting politics, religion, business, education, law and other important social matters, television now takes command. In courtrooms, operating rooms, board rooms, churches and even airplanes, Americans no longer talk to teach other, they entertain each other."[16]

Television's metaphor is nonsequential, transient, visually exciting. It projects rapidly changing, emotion-charged images. We have "image politics" and the television evangelist as celebrity. The church has not used television for a serious purpose, but neither has anyone else. The result is that we Americans are the best entertained but the least-informed people in the world. It is in this milieu that the Christian communicator plies the craft of preaching.

"You Shall Know the Truth . . ."

Although this study as a whole endeavors to interact with such issues, we need to submit certain basic axioms as we begin to clarify where we stand.

The Christian church must, first, be countercultural. The prevailing currents of our time and the physicians of our culture point to the end of the "Age of Exposition," and the mood is all for pluralism, which makes theology a matter of indifference. We cannot go that way. In a time when "authority" is a dirty word, we will stand with biblical authority. We have been told intermittently that preaching has been edged out as far as modern man is

15. Ibid., 79, 80.
16. Ibid., 92.

concerned only to see the effectiveness of mass verbal communication in the raucous 1960s, and I read in my morning paper that the oratory of one of today's politicians "is finding an eager audience." It would be a grave blunder for preachers to jettison the sermon as of negligible value.

Second, we must take seriously our ancient confession, "I believe in the Holy Spirit." Here is where we are strengthened and stabilized for the supernatural enterprise of which we are part. The Holy Spirit is ever in, with, and under the Word. It is the Spirit whose blessing is promised upon the Word to convict of sin, righteousness, and judgment (John 16:8–11). The task of communicating God's wisdom to our age would be impossible apart from the agency of the Spirit of truth. In the next chapter I shall treat our relationship to the Holy Spirit and his role in the life and ministry of the preacher.

Third, in the face of the Herculean challenge of communication in our time, we need to give the utmost attention to discern what adaptations in form and style might contextualize the message to modern listeners without compromising its divinely-given content. The superstructure of this bridge to today's hearers should be supported by these beams:

Preaching should be pictorial. Although some preachers have abandoned "the old conceptual preaching," and many others rely almost exclusively on narrative preaching, some of us have been much too slow to develop skills and expertise in the narrative genre. Theology as story is trendy now; but unfortunately the story so frequently becomes "my" story rather than God's story. Our preaching has become too left-hemispheric—too logical, too analytic, too propositional. These essential elements can be communicated so as to stimulate the brain's right hemisphere, which is creative, imaginative, emotive, and

pictorial. We need more whole-brained thinking, not
what has been called an "unhealthy dictatorship of
the left hemisphere."[17] We will return to this point
in chapter 9.

Preaching should be personal. Charles Haddon Spurgeon used to say that we have never really preached
until we have said "You!" We preach not to the congregation as a whole but to individual persons who
make up the congregation.

Preaching should be practical. The weakest components of contemporary preaching are, tragically
enough, the conclusion and the application. We need
to work much harder on effective running application throughout a sermon, which is more effective than a compacted application at the end. (See
chapter 8 for some guidelines.)

Preaching should be participative. I believe the day of
the manuscript preacher is over. Paper is not a good
conductor of heat. An oral style will foster the sense
of contact between preacher and people. Every taste-
ful way of increasing the sense of sharing dialogue
to the experience is helpful. Sermon talk-backs and
variety in preaching can all be helpful.

Preaching should be pointed. Very few preachers in
America are able to preach more than thirty minutes. My dear wife reminds me that I do not usually
say more in forty-five minutes than I do in thirty
minutes. We must also come to terms with the fact
that listeners are impatient and have brief attention
spans. Even television is making adjustments. Allen
Funt of the series "Candid Camera" reports that he
used to produce episodes five minutes long. Now
they average two and one-half minutes. "Do it and

17. Herbert Benson, *Your Maximum Mind* (New York: Times Books, 1987);
Stanley L. Englebardt, "Are You Thinking Right?" *Reader's Digest* 132 (February 1988): 41–45.

go," Funt says.[18] With P. T. Forsyth we may lament our "fatal urgency for brevity," but it is only wise and sensible for us to recognize that the Puritans preached in a different age. Matters of form and style that are cultural traditions rather than biblical mandates can be adapted.

Fourth, preaching needs to fit into the design of the whole worship experience. The resurgence of interest in worship holds great promise for the upbuilding of the body of Christ and the praise of our God, and it also relates to the preaching challenge in our time. Too frequently have we thought of the sermon apart from the worship service. Some of us low churchmen and devotees of a free liturgy have even used descriptives such as "opening exercises" and "preliminaries" to describe the worship service. While the sermon is the climax of worship, it is an integral part of an organismic whole. Exciting things are happening in worship among us, and this augurs well for preaching.

The careful planning of worship around a theme with movement and pacing is a great challenge. Orthodox worship is like a drama, repeating and portraying divine history in the great redemptive acts of God. Some in the renewal mode of Protestantism even include an occasional dramatic segment to raise the issue to be faced. Wherever we find ourselves liturgically, the concept that the sermon is a part of the worship service as a whole opens vast horizons of possibility.

The need to exegete our culture is a fifth consideration. Just as the preacher must faithfully and diligently exegete the text which is to be preached, so the preacher must exegete the thought patterns and value systems which mold and shape the apperceptive background of the listeners. As he shepherds his people, the sensitive

18. Philip B. Zimbardo, "Laugh Where We Must, Be Candid Where We Can," *Psychology Today* 19 (June 1985): 47.

pastor will pick up certain nuances which will give small brush strokes to the need. But the broader canvas needs to be studied. Books such as *Habits of the Heart*, in which Robert N. Bellah and several co-authors study the quality of American spiritual commitment, show us, for example, that "feeling good" has replaced "being good."[19] *Crumbling Foundations* by Donald G. Bloesch or *Megatruth* by David McKenna are examples of substantial studies which help the communicator get close to the wellsprings of modern life and thought.[20] James D. Hunter's *Evangelicalism* is also a sobering in-depth analysis, and Richard J. Neuhaus in *The Naked Public Square* provides a thoughtful reflection on religion in public life in America today.[21] Ongoing study affords the preacher a realistic understanding of who his auditors are and where they are. We need help to tell us if we are answering questions no one is really asking and why the right questions aren't being asked.

In a fast-moving and breathless age, the biblical preacher need not be moved off vital center or make mindless and meaningless accommodations to the latest rage. Yet the modern communications revolution allows none of us to sit back complacently. There is a compelling need for the preacher to consider what we are doing and how we could do it better for the glory of God and the good of the church.

---

19. Robert N. Bellah et al., *Habits of the Heart: Individualism and Commitment in American Life* (Berkeley, Calif.: University of California Press, 1985).

20. Donald G. Bloesch, *Crumbling Foundations: Death and Rebirth in an Age of Upheaval* (Grand Rapids: Zondervan, 1984); David McKenna, *Megatruth: The Church in the Age of Information* (San Bernardino, Calif.: Here's Life, 1987).

21. James D. Hunter, *Evangelicalism: The Coming Generation* (Chicago: University of Chicago Press, 1987); Richard J. Neuhaus, *The Naked Public Square: Religion and Democracy in America* (Grand Rapids: Eerdmans, 1984).

4

What Is Happening to the Preachers?
The Issue of Spirituality

We will proceed no further on the subject of preaching without giving some attention to the preacher. The text which was preached at my ordination has lingered hauntingly for a lifetime: "Watch your life and doctrine closely" (1 Tim. 4:16). The inspired apostle insists: "Therefore, since through God's mercy we have this ministry, we do not lose heart. Rather, we have renounced secret and shameful ways; we do not use deception, nor do we distort the word of God" (2 Cor. 4:1–2). The character of the preacher and the nature of his or her spiritual walk are inextricably bound up with the preaching event.

Aristotle has a good deal to say about the character of the speaker in his *Rhetoric*. Matters of the personality, preparation, and attitudes of the speaker bear significantly upon discourse. The prime importance of character is indicated in Aristotle's insistence that "persuasion is achieved by the speaker's personal character when the speech is so spoken as to make us think him credible. We believe good men more fully and readily than others: this is true generally whatever the question is, and absolutely true where exact certainty is impossible and opinions are divided."[1]

Preaching the truth of God is not done without reference to the life and experience of the human communicator. This is not to say that the Spirit of God may not be pleased in signal instances to bless the Word of God even when articulated by some rascal or scalawag. In a celebrated instance even Balaam's jackass was the chosen instrument!

But it is curious and most lamentable that so many basic textbooks in homiletics and academic courses in preaching virtually ignore the vital aspects of the spirituality of the preacher. This is but one more sign that spirituality has been largely banished from Protestant theological education until quite recently. The formation of character and community has been preempted by concerns for the development of skills and competencies required for ministry today. One of the most heartening developments in relation to the preaching task is the renewal of interest in Christian spirituality in the church. The reissuance of great classics and a cascade of new titles bear witness to the vitality of this surge; it is reflected in new emphases in many seminaries and training schools. Several recent issues of *Theological Education,* published by The Association of Theological Schools, wrestle with this crucial aspect of preparing ministers spiritually for their task.[2] The preacher of the Word is not a salesman or a showman; he is a spokesman! Hence our theology of proclamation must be closely wed to our theology of devotion.

1. Aristotle, *Rhetoric* 1.2, 4–5, trans. W. Rhys Roberts, in *Great Books of the Western World,* ed. Robert M. Hutchins and Mortimer Adler, 54 vols. (Chicago: Encyclopaedia Britannica, 1952), 9, 2: 595.

2. The Association of Theological Schools, *Theological Education* 24 (Autumn 1987); Supplement to Autumn 1987. Part 1 of the Autumn 1987 issue was devoted to the topic "Spirituality in Theological Education." Further essays and interest induced the editors to publish a supplemental issue in early 1988 on the topic "Theological Education as the Formation of Character."

No one has put it more concisely or compellingly than Benjamin B. Warfield: "What we need in our pulpits is scholar-saints become preachers. And it is the one business of the theological seminaries to make them."[3] The preacher must be nurtured not only in a nursery of learning but also in a nursery of piety. Augustine's dictum is essentially correct: "What I live by, I impart." John Newton said, "None but He who made the world can make a minister." Cotton Mather subtitled his volume for ministerial students, "The angels preparing to sound the trumpets."[4]

Lyle E. Schaller's recent volume, *It's a Different World*,[5] explains why the inner spiritual dynamics are so vital now. Fundamental shifts are taking place in society and parish life which make being a pastor harder today than it was thirty years ago. At the forefront of the spiritual battle, the pastor-preacher now finds that television has provided his congregants with a new base of comparison. Much fiercer competition, erosion of traditional loyalties, less homogeneity in the congregation, and the multiplication of options due to our affluence all put new emphasis on the competence, personality, and performance of the minister.

The Preacher and Identity in Christ

The work of Erik H. Erikson and others on identity formation has demonstrated that an inadequate inner base can cripple a person with acute self-consciousness and cause a tendency toward brittleness and ineptitude

3. Benjamin B. Warfield, "The Purpose of the Seminary," in *The Selected Shorter Writings of Benjamin B. Warfield*, 2 vols., ed. John E. Meeter (Nutley, N.J.: Presbyterian and Reformed, 1970), 1:378.

4. Benjamin B.Warfield, "The Religious Life of Theological Students," in *Selected Shorter Writings*, 1:425.

5. Lyle E. Schaller, *It's a Different World: The Challenge for Today's Pastor* (Nashville: Abingdon, 1987).

in the realm of the interpersonal.[6] On the other hand,
"Jesus knew that the Father had put all things under
his power, and that he had come from God and was
returning to God; so he got up from the meal, took off his
outer clothing, and wrapped a towel around his waist"
(John 13:3–4). The Savior's poise and purposefulness
rose out of his sense of who he was and a harmonious
and right relationship with his Father.

An alumni survey conducted by Trinity Evangelical
Divinity School indicated that graduates wish they had
received more assistance in their student days in the
areas of self-understanding, self-assessment, evaluating
strengths and weaknesses, and in the culture of the inner
life. The increasing incidence of clergy burnout accen-
tuates awareness of the mounting pressures of the broad-
ening task and expanding expectations focused on clergy.

Some of us are too introspective and hyperconscien-
tious. In Arnold A. Dallimore's two-volume biography of
George Whitefield is the constant staccato of Whitefield's
inner struggle: "O that I may begin to be in earnest," he
groans. "Every week I cry out—my leanness! my leanness!" "Surely I am a worthless worm!" "I do not deserve
even the rank of a common soldier in Christ's army."[7]
Excessive anguish of this kind can be debilitating.

Some of us are more prone to "the inflated self" with
all of its self-serving bias. In either extreme, it is the
gospel which helps to free us from self-obsession. In
Christ I face my infinite capacity for self-deception, for
at the cross of Christ I must own my sins and the per-
versity of my fallen nature. It is here that I find deliverance and relief through the forgiveness of all my sins

    6. Erik H. Erikson, *Identity, Youth and Crises* (New York: W. W. Norton,
1968).
    7. Arnold A. Dallimore, *George Whitefield: The Life and Times of the Great
Evangelist of the Eighteenth-Century Revival* (London: Banner of Truth, 1970),
see especially 86–87.

through the blood of Jesus and become a new person in Christ.

Be my problem the exacting demands of a highly developed superego and its resultant compulsive perfectionism or low self-worth, my right to preach and represent a holy God does not depend on my own meritorious good works any more than does my eternal salvation. I have seen the glory of the Lord, I have confessed that I am unclean and undone, and my sin has been purged (as in Isaiah 6, the paradigm of a prophet's call). My own inner impoverishment of self-confidence or my lack of external attractiveness or superior endowment all must yield to the decisive determinant of my essential identity—I am accepted in Christ and am being healed.

> My sin—O the joy of this glorious thought;
> My sin, not in part, but the whole,
> Is nailed to the cross and I bear it no more:
> Praise the Lord, praise the Lord, O my soul!
> —Horatio G. Spafford

This deep inner assurance of sin's forgiveness and what it means to be "justified freely by his grace through the redemption which is in Christ Jesus" (Rom. 3:24) provides the matrix for the preacher's identity and sense of call and enablement.

The Preacher and the Word

Prime Minister David Lloyd George of England said, "When the chariot of humanity gets stuck in the mud, nothing will lift it out but strong Biblical preaching that goes straight to the heart and mind." The regimen required for the faithful and steady "ministry of the Word" is formidable and demanding. If we are to feed others we ourselves must be fed. If we are going to give out, we must be replenished and filled. In *Pilgrim's Progress,* when Christian came to the House of Interpreter he was shown many wonderful things, including "the picture of a very grave person hung up against the wall; and this was the fashion of it: it had eyes lifted up to heaven, the best of books was in his hand, the law of truth was upon his lips, the world was behind his back; it stood as if it pleaded with men, and a crown of gold did hang over its head." This is John Bunyan's metaphor of the Christian minister as a man of the Word. Only as this Word is truly hidden in our hearts will we be able to declare its truth to others with authority and grace.

Everything else in personal piety and ministry stands in relation to a vital, daily life in the Scripture. John A. Broadus, the redoubtable Southern Baptist New Testament scholar and homiletician, in his last lecture placed great stress that preachers seek to be "mighty in the Scriptures" (Acts 18:24 KJV). This means more than vigorous and disciplined exegesis of texts in the interest of the sermons they will yield. This means a diligent personal and devotional study of the Book. Interestingly, the most prestigious center for Muslim studies in the world is al-Azhar University in Cairo, Egypt, which has thirty thousand students. The prerequisite for study there is the ability to recite the Koran by heart.[8] The Koran has 114 suras or chapters and seventy-eight thousand words. This is a measure of the discipline and devotion of others.

Martin Luther testified that his study of the Word was like gathering apples. He shook the whole tree so that the ripest might fall. Then he climbed the tree and shook each limb, then each branch, and then each twig. Then, he said, he looked under each leaf. The preacher needs that kind of excitement and enthusiasm in the Word of God. A congregation soon senses whether the preacher is making fresh, new discoveries in the Scripture, bringing out treasures old and new.

---

8. Wilhelm Dietz, *Holy War* (New York: Macmillan, 1984), 108–9.

Psalm 119 is a garden of meditations on the Word of God about which Franz Delitzsch maintained, "Here we have set forth in inexhaustible fulness what the Word of God is to us, and how we are to behave ourselves in relation to it."[9] This psalm contains 183 references to the Word (using eight different titles for Scripture). A study of the verbs used to describe our approach to revealed truth in God's Word shows that we are to seek, to rejoice, to meditate (to attend with intention; remember that the preoccupation of our time, "to amuse," literally means "not to think"), to keep, to choose, to long for, to love, to delight, to remember, to consider, and to hide in our hearts.

Our Lord Jesus knew the Word, trusted the Word, loved the Word, and used the Word. It is always the privilege of the student of Scripture to be in the presence of the divine author. As a Charles Dickens buff, I have read Dickens, mastered his biography, visited related sites in Britain, and belonged to the Charles Dickens Fellowship. But I have no interpersonal contact or concourse with Dickens himself. Yet it is my exquisite joy daily to be in the very presence of my God and to track and trace his truth with his help and guidance. "Oh, how I love your law!" Whatever other books and materials we may pursue or master, this is *The Book*.

The Preacher and Prayer

Strange it is that any discussion of preaching could take place outside the context of believing prayer. We have not prepared until we have prayed. Karl Barth has said, "If there is no great agony in our hearts, there will be no great words on our lips." The principle here is the often-repeated fact: "No one has the power of God with men unless he has power with God for men." Yet studies

9. Franz J. Delitzsch, *Bible Commentary on the Psalms,* 2nd ed. rev., translated by Francis Bolton (Grand Rapids: Eerdmans, 1949).

show that a lukewarm devotional life is considered the most serious problem parish pastors face on a daily basis. William Hulme asked twelve hundred Lutheran ministers in the United States to name the areas of ministry giving them the greatest satisfaction and the greatest dissatisfaction. Sixty-five percent were bothered by their devotional life, and 50 percent said their lack of devotional life caused them serious stress. Hulme argues that a devotional or prayer life gives one a focus or a center from which one can analyze life—identity.[10] It has to take priority.

We cannot represent God if we have not stood before God. It is more important for me therefore to teach a student to pray than to preach. The avalanche of books on the subject of prayer reminds us that it is easier to talk about prayer than it is to pray, yet prayer makes such a difference that a situation is never the same after we have prayed about it. There is so much I do not understand about prayer—I am increasingly a mystic regarding it. Yet an inductive study of what the Bible says about prayer reinforces Blaise Pascal's conviction that "God has established prayer to give us a taste of what it means to be a creator."

What we really believe is shown by how we pray. John Wesley said of his daily time with God, "I am so busy I cannot spend less than two hours in prayer." Jesus said, "Could you not watch with me one hour?" (Matt. 26:40). Robert Murray McCheyne urged his people to turn the Bible into prayer, and as a result more than thirty prayer meetings met weekly in his parish of Dundee, Scotland, five of which were children's prayer meetings.

David Brainerd shared what prayer with a small cadre of Christians meant to him: "I prayed privately with a dear Christian friend or two; and I think I scarce ever launched so far out on the broad ocean that my soul with

10. William E. Hulme, *Pastors in Ministry: Guidelines for Seven Critical Issues* (Minneapolis: Augsburg, 1985).

joy triumphed over all the evils on the shores of mortality. I think that time and all its gay amusements and cruel disappointments never appeared so inconsiderable to me before." John Henry Jowett had a place of prayer. For this prince of preachers it was an upper room in his house. In this room were two chairs; one was always vacant. There was a table in this room and nothing else except the Bible on the table. Jowett would sit in one chair, read the Word, and talk with the Lord. It is said that he spent hours with his Master thus in deep and sweet communion.

Charles Haddon Spurgeon attributed the signal blessing of God upon his ministry in London to the faithfulness of his people to pray for him. The story has often been told of the five college students who came to hear Spurgeon preach at the Metropolitan Tabernacle. While waiting for the doors to open, they were greeted by a gentleman who offered to show them around. "Would you like to see the heating plant?" he inquired. They were not particularly interested because it was a hot day in July. Nonetheless they followed him down a staircase where he opened a door, whispering: "This is our heating plant." The surprised students saw seven hundred people bowed in prayer, interceding for the service about to begin upstairs and for their beloved pastor. Softly closing the door, the gentleman then introduced himself to them. It was Spurgeon.

A worshiper at Free Saint George's West in Edinburgh came up to Alexander Whyte after a particularly stirring message and exclaimed: "Dr. Whyte, you preached today like you had just emerged from the throne chamber of the Almighty," to which Whyte replied, "In point of fact, I have." The secrets of the hidden life of prayer and fasting are to be sought by those who would preach "not simply in words, but also with power, with the Holy Spirit and with deep conviction" (1 Thess. 1:5). We need to acquaint ourselves with the solitudes and altitudes

known to a George Müller, a Hudson Taylor, an Andrew
Murray, a Rees Howells, or an Armin Gesswein. "Lord,
teach us to pray."

The Preacher and the Holy Spirit

The apostle Paul's reflection on his preaching needs to
be ours: "My message and my preaching were not with
wise and persuasive words, but with a demonstration of
the Spirit's power, so that your faith might not rest on
men's wisdom, but on God's power" (1 Cor. 2:4–5). What
brings conviction to our placid pools of prose? What
ensures that pregnant ideas are born in powerful delivery? Gimmicks won't do it—swinging out of the gallery
on a guy wire with a rose in your mouth won't do it. It
is the renewal and fullness of the blessed Holy Spirit that
makes our preaching come alive.

Evidence of what I have termed a fresh stirring of
interest in Christian spirituality is the publication of a
choice volume, *Preaching in the Spirit,* by Dennis Kinlaw
of Asbury College in Wilmore, Kentucky. This book treats
the necessity of our total reliance on the ministry of the
Holy Spirit, quoting Albert B. Simpson that "we are
empty possibilities until He gets us."[11]

It strikes me that the ministry of the Holy Spirit
relates to the preaching task in at least four aspects:

1. *The Spirit gives help in preparation.* He came to
   guide us into truth. After Pentecost the disciples of
   Jesus had understanding.
2. *The Spirit gives courage in anticipation.* Preaching
   is such an audacious enterprise. How was Peter,
   who had crumbled so catastrophically, up to facing
   that vast throng with such boldness and bravery?
   He was filled with the Spirit.

11. Dennis Kinlaw, *Preaching in the Spirit* (Grand Rapids: Francis Asbury,
1985), 62.

3. *The Spirit gives inspiration in presentation.* Our total dependency on the Spirit is harrowing, as is visualized in Zechariah 4:1–14. When Bunyan preached in seventeenth-century London, he drew audiences greater than the learned divines because he preached with such obvious power. The well-known John Owen was often in attendance. When Charles II expressed his astonishment that a man of Owen's learning could hear "the tinker preach," Owen is said to have replied, "Had I the tinker's abilities, please Your Majesty, I would gladly relinquish my learning."[12]

4. *The Spirit gives follow-up in implementation.* Who pursues the good seed which has been sown? In every way our auditors go, the Holy Spirit continues his gracious office work.

At every stage and juncture the claimant need is for the control and filling of the Holy Spirit. A person is filled with the Spirit to the degree that one is controlled by the Spirit, sharing both his gifts and his graces. "Keep on being filled with the Spirit" (Eph. 5:18 [author's translation]). This is the preaching which is under the anointing, not in the sand of the flesh but in the oil of the Holy Ghost.

The Preacher and Personal Holiness

Time magazine has spoken of "evangelicalism's tattered image." As this is written the ministry has been widely discredited by sordid scandals. Acculturated evangelicalism has been heading for a fall, and, painful as is the purging, our God "makes even the wrath of men to praise him!" We have all needed the humbling and the shaking we have received as an agonizing reminder that

12. Gardiner Spring, *The Power of the Pulpit* (1848; reprint ed., Carlisle, Pa.: Banner of Truth, 1986).

we must live looking to Jesus (Heb. 12:1–2). The sense of
the reality of the Lord keeps confidence from becoming
arrogance. The fact that Jesus came to save us from our
sins (Matt. 1:21) should make a demonstrable difference
between the church and the world. Paul was enabled to
say through the sanctifying grace of the Lord Jesus
Christ, "You know how I lived the whole time I was with
you" (Acts 20:18). Inscribed on the tomb of Basil (c. 329–
379), bishop of Caesarea, was the epitaph, "His words
were thunder, his life lightning." McCheyne used to say,
"My people's greatest need is for my own personal holiness."

Yet sin dwells deep within us. D. L. Moody said of one
young preacher he heard, "There's too much of the toma-
hawk in him." Overly feisty and combative preachers ill-
disguise resistant areas of their inner life. A trenchant
observation by the biographer of Gilbert Tennent (1703–
1764) shines the light deep into all of our souls: "Tennent's ego was subject to the same overweening pride
that Whitefield, Zinzendorf, and many of the other great
figures of the contemporary American and English reviv-
als on occasion exhibited."[13]

Thus we are "called to holiness," to waft the fragrance
of our Savior to those about us in kindly, compassionate,
upright lives of purity and integrity. This is the daily
battle against the world, the flesh, and the devil, in
which we put on the articles of the "whole armor of God."
This is to enter into the deliverance promised us in
Romans 6, where we read that "sin shall not be your
master" (Rom. 6:14). While justification is instantaneous,
sanctification proceeds toward maturity (Heb. 6:1–3), a
growing "in the grace and knowledge of our Lord and
Savior Jesus Christ" (2 Pet. 3:18). As Oswald Chambers
put it so trenchantly, "Sanctification is allowing the per-

13. Milton J. Coalter, *Gilbert Tennent: Son of Thunder* (New York: Green-
wood, 1986).

fections of the Lord Jesus to express themselves in human personality."

Alfred Lord Tennyson described "the sin whose practice burns in the blood." George Bernanos spoke of how we breathe in sin with the very atmosphere. Yet we are called to win the battle in the thought life, to bring "every thought captive to Christ." One day when he was rather discouraged, Frederick W. Robertson visited a shopkeeper who belonged to the church. The shopkeeper showed him a picture of Robertson on the wall. He said that whenever he was tempted to sell someone shoddy goods, he looked at his pastor's picture and was strengthened to do right. May such a beautiful work of grace be wrought in your and my hearts that we may be truly able ministers of the new covenant.

5

Where Are We Going with Structure?
The Issue of Morphology

Paul E. Johnson's powerful history, *Modern Times,* opens with the assertion that on one spring day in 1919 the world of Newtonian physics, with its eminently comprehensible straight lines and right angles, was forced to give way to Albert Einstein's relativistic or nonstructured universe.[1] The reaction against structure in our times can be seen in the protest against Georg F. W. Hegel's sense of system in which sequence is so critical. Søren Kierkegaard and existentialists, as well as pragmatists and logical positivists, have all argued against structure. This is the age of Lloyd Morgan's emergent evolution with its unpredictability and Werner K. Heisenberg's principle of indeterminacy. We see the mood in stream-of-consciousness novels and the theater of the absurd. The general abandonment of coherence and structure in the arts finds ultimate expression in Jacques Derrida and the literary "deconstructionists" who now hold sway in places like Yale University and

1. Paul E. Johnson, *Modern Times: The World from the Twenties to the Eighties* (New York: Harper and Row, 1983), 1.

who go so far as to argue that grammar is fascist and that we cannot know the mind of the author. This is the abandonment of any normative understanding of the text. "We make up the steps as we go along."[2]

There is truth in the notions that beauty analyzed is beauty destroyed, that "we murder to dissect," and that it is tragically reductionistic to maintain that a rational definition of love suffices. We nonetheless lament many of the results of the reaction against structure which are to be seen in the crafting of sermons in our time. The preacher must move from the exegesis of the text to the shaping of the sermon. The central proposition derived from the text and developed with supporting material must be packaged for communication. The content must be given form. The classical and traditional mode has been to project a series of main ideas and subpoints to carry the argument. Augustine insisted that both sequentia and eloquentia are needed in effective discourse, a process classical rhetoric regards as *invention* (the ideas) moving on to *arrangement* or *disposition* (the ordering of the ideas). Demosthenes recognized that persuasion depends as much on the order of presentation as on the strength of the argument.

Preaching has historically overemphasized the parts, making of the preacher a lecturer whose fine-lined analysis too easily became the end in itself. John A. Broadus speaks of "the excessive multiplication of formal divisions and equally formal sub-divisions."[3] The syllogistic model, the stereotypical three points and a poem, triumphed. Such a neoscholastic overemphasis on structure produced many infirmities in preaching, including the highly ornate French-lacquer sermon.

The general cultural reaction against structure and

2. Bryce Christensen, "Clipping the Angel's Wings," *Chronicles of Culture* 10, 12 (December 1986): 23.

3. John A. Broadus, *On the Preparation and Delivery of Sermons* (San Francisco: Harper and Row, 1979), 89.

Victorian excess was about even a century ago when Matthew Arnold argued that the sermon should be more of an informal address without divisions as such. In more modern terms the watchword became "Away with canned homiletics" where all is sliced and diced; the old forms are inadequate and inappropriate linear Aristotelian thinking. The result has been that many preachers develop what must be called an oral essay. The tendency is that pools of literary protoplasm are loosed to flow in all directions simultaneously. This is the river sermon which winds about like the Meander. Such a format fits this era of hesitation in the twilight of authority, but is it at all satisfying if we would apply "thus saith the Lord" to the studied ambiguities of our time? I make no brief here for unadaptive forms, but the *disjecta membra* (scattered parts) of much modern preaching lead us nowhere.

We shall argue here for holistic communication, a Gestalt pattern with a strong statement of main points and a deliberate deemphasis on the statement of subpoints. A model might be the tree, with trunk, branches, and twigs as a living and organic whole with beauty and symmetry; or it may be seen as an offspring, a baby rather than a building. The Reverend Canon Charles Minifie, president of the College of Preachers in Washington, D. C., observed that the pendulum is swinging back to "a return to the older ways of putting together sermons; we are no longer so beguiled by communication theories that grew up in the academic world under the impact of television."[4]

The Case for Structure

There is preaching which could be described as a maze without a plan. It may even be an unilluminating dis-

---

4. "Lessons in Deliverance of the Word," *Insight* 3, 43 (October 26, 1987): 54.

cussion of unreal problems in unintelligible language. The result is like throwing an egg into an electric fan. A sermon must have both shape and content. Ronald E. Sleeth spoke about dismissing linear thought with all of its limitations, but he agreed with Roger Copeland, the dramatist, that the linear and the Aristotelian still have "distinctive theatrical power, waiting to be tapped like so much fissionable material approaching critical mass."[5] Sleeth concluded that there must be movement and progression in the sermon. Even David G. Buttrick, who presides over what he hopes will be the dismantling of the old homiletic, concedes that "all speaking involves sequence."[6] If a sermon is to be more than an artful souffle, the proper arrangement of form is important. Substance and form affect each other, however. Each of Paul's sermons develops a theme around a single thought. Aristotle long ago opined that beauty depends on order and magnitude. There must be some magnitude to organize, for the elaboration of a trifle is still a trifle. The unctuous elaboration of the obvious makes no positive contribution. It makes the preacher resemble a hippopotamus chasing after a pea.

More than twenty lecturers in the annual Beecher Lecture series at Yale have concentrated on organizing and arranging the sermon for greater effectiveness. Some will scorn the "1–2–3 stuff," but there must be method whereby the progress and movement of the action can be measured. Just as in sports, there are necessary lines and demarcations. The main points in the sermon are like successive golf shots to reach the green. There is more to be said in favor of clearly stating main points than is to be said against it. Alvin C. Rueter calls clarity "the handle factor" to help people get a grip on the ser-

5. Ronald E. Sleeth, *God's Word and Our Words: Basic Homiletics* (Atlanta: John Knox, 1986), 49.

6. David G. Buttrick, *Homiletic: Moves and Structures* (Philadelphia: Fortress, 1987), 309.

mon.[7] If the handle should be invisible it is nonfunctional. The statement of the mains supplies for the listening audience what the heads in a newspaper article or book supply to the reader. These are indispensable for communication. The sea creature who assays to walk on dry land without skeletal endowment will collapse gelatinously, as Halford Luccock has pointed out.

Austin Phelps maintained that the sermon is a structure and that classifying materials tends to unify them. Blaise Pascal observed that "good thoughts abound, but the art of organizing them does not." Gerald Kennedy felt that lack of organization is the greatest weakness in preaching today. We more easily learn material that is organized, so there is greater power in organized thought. In the disconnectedness of modern life, there is also a great craving for a sense of order and connection, as there is a need for our God of order. A clear, poignant statement of this unmet need on the personal level was made by "Rebecca," a woman whose difficult emotional problems were described by Oliver Sacks. Looking down at the office carpet, Rebecca said to her therapist: "I am like a sort of living carpet. I need a pattern, a design, like you have on that carpet. I come apart, I unravel, unless there's a design."[8] So too the sermon must have a design.

The sermon also must have a destination in view, unlike the arrow shot into the air: "It fell to earth, I know not where." Clovis Chappell used to say that the sermon should be like a journey—you start, you travel, you arrive. This is what structure makes possible.

That structure needs an outline, with clearly set out main points. Jean Claude (1619–1687), the French

7. Alvin C. Rueter, "Issues Shaping Effective Proclamation," *Emphasis* 14 (February 1985): 9.

8. Oliver Sacks, *The Man Who Mistook His Wife for a Hat and Other Clinical Tales* (New York: Harper and Row, 1987), 184.

Huguenot preacher, in his essay on "The Composition of a Sermon" recognizes that the divisions of the biblical text should be reflected in the divisions of the sermon to be preached on the text. These divisions should be few in number, never more than four or five and preferably two or three. Some students of the craft have a difficult time in outlining so there should be much practice and application at this point, because outlining the mains is crucial. Too many points weaken the main point. It is also well for the structure to show, but not to be too bony, like a famine victim. Make those mains stand out, each word receiving full, strong emphasis. If the skeletal form seems too prominent or protrusive, the answer is not to remove the structure but rather to clothe it with living tissue.

In sum, the reaction against structure has been disastrous for preaching, but we can never go back to the artificial rigidities out of which we have come. The didactic sermon needs a clear outline with no enumeration of the subs. Certain more innovative forms and the narrative sermon, now so much in vogue, have entirely different ground rules, which will be discussed in subsequent chapters. Strong as is my attachment to a clear and cogent sense of design in the didactic portions of Scripture, I realize that I need another model or paradigm for the narrative. Here we have a greater range of options and an entirely different genre. But in every case responsiveness to the text should determine structure.

The New Homiletic

It was only a matter of time before the new hermeneutic should be followed by the new homiletic. The work of Buttrick has already been critiqued for its flawed view of Scripture, but it is "must" reading for the serious student of the craft. Buttrick is a demolitionist but he still holds that "sermons involve an ordered sequence."[9] He arches his homiletical back, however, at what he feels is too punctilious an approach to structure in traditional homiletic. We would readily concur that much preaching is too boxy. It is in chunks and gobs, parts and pieces. He proposes that, instead of speaking of points in the sermon, we refer to "moves." Already in that metaphor we sense something fluid. Instead of the outline we have the plot, and instead of the proposition, we have the intention. There is an idea of significance here.

The old conceptual preaching is outmoded, Buttrick essentially argues. We have a much shorter time span and we must use image. "Designing moves involves theological smarts and rhetorical skill," he asserts.[10] Like a point, a coherent move opens, develops, and closes. Yet the move is more strictly structured with no more than three internal parts. The great danger is fragmenting the move and splitting the field of consciousness, which is basically the listener's frame of reference.

Buttrick opposes enumeration of moves because this introduces time-consciousness and induces restlessness. Eschewing traditional transitions, he wants connection which does not obliterate the distinctive identity of each move. How this is substantively different from our desire for smooth transition is not altogether clear. He is adamantly opposed to preannouncing the plot. "Destruction of suspense is positively unkind."[11]

Personal narrative is, strangely enough, taboo. Buttrick's objection is the danger of splitting the focus. One example is allocated for each move and never more than three chained examples. Similarly, one illustration is allowed for each move. The alignment of the illustration with the strength of the move is strongly emphasized. Buttrick stresses the importance of the right fit of an

9. Buttrick, *Homiletic,* 23.
10. Ibid., 28.
11. Ibid., 85.

illustration to what it illustrates. Crucial moves need to be illustrated; compressed images in the common field of consciousness aptly achieve their purpose.[12]

Buttrick crusades against static points in the sermon, and yet he wants the sermon's bones to show. His aversion to any idea of the fixed authority of Scripture makes the very subjective present field of consciousness the point of decisive determination.[13] His book itself lacks any footnotes to document sweeping allegations, a demonstration of how he revels in living without authority at all. As he says, "We are not breaking a text into a sermon, but rather replotting a field of understanding into a sermon—a contemporary sermon."[14] Indeed we may not use a text or draw upon Scripture at all. The meaning in contemporary consciousness totally commands a field of human hermeneutics. The preacher stands in tragic agnosticism before Scripture instead of approaching the sacred text with appropriate humility. In Buttrick's view it is necessary, though, for the "meaning of texts now is difficult to discern."[15] The new hermeneutic has come to full flower in the new homiletic. There are some extraordinarily helpful insights to be found here on aspects of structure in relation to communication today, but essentially this is to receive a stone when we need bread.

Dividing the Central Proposition

The Logical Outline

Our first responsibility is to find what the text means and then to preach what it says. The purpose of the mains is to develop and argue the central idea or proposition of the sermon. The mains need to stand in an

12. Ibid., 70.
13. Ibid., 248.
14. Ibid., 312.
15. Ibid., 243.

obvious and clear relationship to the theme being developed. Examples where this is *not* the case illustrate the point:

On Genesis 1:1
  I. God created the earth
  II. God created the earth with three-fourths water
  III. I infer a baptismal purpose

On the text, "Balaam rose early and saddled his ass"
  I. A good trait in a bad character
  II. The antiquity of saddlery
  III. A few thoughts on the woman of Samaria[16]

In casting the mains, beware of using the homiletical cookie cutter. Vary the number. Three mains are most popular. Using more than four or five mains is not really feasible. Frederick W. Robertson and Walter A. Meier invariably used two mains, usually the problem/solution pattern. John Chrysostom usually employed three divisions, John Calvin ordinarily had two, and Alexander Maclaren used three natural, memorable divisions. Henry P. Liddon used three heads, and Charles Haddon Spurgeon's textual sermons used Aristotelian subdivisions.

The very statement of the mains is an important skill to develop. While sentences, clauses, and single words can be used for the statement of the mains, complete sentences with both subject and predicate are more assertive. We establish a significant beachhead in our argument with a full, assertive sentence. The declarative sentence is the best, with occasional use of the imperative. Too much imperative is heavy for a congregation. The exhortation and admonition will come in finishing the point or move, so it is best not to cast the main itself in the imperative. The use of the name of God is always

16. Donald Kroll, *Prescription for Preaching* (Grand Rapids: Baker, 1980).

appropriate; but it is preferable not to use proper names from Bible times since these create distance in time between the text and its hearers. Use of the first person plural tends to bring the audience into the action. The mains should be discrete, that is, mutually exclusive. There will be real problems in the development if two of the mains are just different ways of stating the same truth. The mains should be grammatically parallel. Thoughtful and careful use of alliteration or assonance may assist both preacher and auditor to remember the outline. The best use of art is to conceal the art.

There is an art to plotting main points which bring life to the sermon—art which communicates. Sometimes what we call "plot clot" is due to fuzziness in stating the main. Archbishop James Ussher observed that it takes all of our learning to make things plain. Dr. Obvious may try to preach the following outline, but the points are too narrow gauge:

 I. Moses was a great man.
 II. Moses was a good man.
 III. Moses was a wise man.

Performative discourse and participative action are at the heart of biblical communication. The use of the past tense, proper names from the long-ago, and weak verbs with platitudinous adjectives doom it. The young preacher ordinarily attempts too much and the result is sprawl. Learn to delimit. As Ronald Ward loved to put it, "The sermon after all is a monograph, not the encyclopedia." Note also in the outline about Moses that no text is actually used. This sermon would tend to be moralistic in tone. If indeed the text had scarlet fever, the sermon would not catch it.

H. Grady Davis in *Design for Preaching* is helpful on how to develop the thought under the mains. He insists

that "great preaching is always in the present tense."[17]
The Bible is not an antique factory. We can become
trapped in the text itself, in that we never get out of the
ancient world and its situations. Davis pleads with us
not to give our people the chips we make in carving the
statue, but the statue itself. He reminds us that the first
words our Lord Jesus spoke publicly were in the present
tense: "*Today* this Scripture is fulfilled in your hearing"
(Luke 4:21, emphasis added).

I like to keep a sheet with the different types of sermon
outlines on it at hand when I come to projecting the statement of my mains. Broadus has a good list, as do others.
Such creative terms as "the ladder," "the diamond," "the
problem/solution," "the guessing game," "the dialectic,"
"the dog fight," and "the subversive" describe different
patterns which can be used to good advantage.

The Emotional Outline

Beyond the logical outline is the seldom considered
emotional outline. Indolent repetition of old phrases flat-
tens a sermon hopelessly. Monomood delivery will give
no sense of peaks and valleys. There need to be moments
of effective intensity and then a backing off and moments
of relief for the congregation. Working at half throttle all
the time won't do, nor will going full bore throughout
delivery, like lightning which flashes all over but strikes
nowhere.

Sermons sag for lack of an emotional outline. Quite
common is a starburst of enthusiasm in a long and strong
first main. The second main is five minutes shorter, and
the last main is just a momentary shot and whistle. The
emotional curve is down. We need to balance out the
mains. The first and last require special care. There is
an emotional rhythm in preaching which is especially
dominant in preaching in the black church. Here what

17. H. Grady Davis, *Design for Preaching* (Philadelphia: Muhlenberg,
1958), 203.

is called "hooping" is an integral part of the traditional black pattern. Hooping is the rhythmic response and answer of the congregation to the preacher's mounting crescendo of emotion. It is a magnificent kind of dialogue seldom experienced outside of the black church.

Ralph Waldo Emerson is reputed to have said of a series of lectures he had given: "A cold, mechanical preparation. . . . [F]ine things, pretty things, wise things, but no arrows, no axes, no nectar, no growling, no transpiercing, no loving, no enchantment." This describes an experience we have all had in preaching. Lack of ignition may be caused by something in our own hearts or our own preparation or in the congregation. Yet it can be the consequence of our structure. The emotional outline can be skewed or distorted because of faulty mains. We may, for instance, have a first main which explodes so dynamically that the rest is down hill. This may require devaluing the first main or restating and rearranging our material. It is occasionally possible to hear an illustration early on in the sermon which is so forceful that it blows the rest of the message out of the water. It may be too much at any point, but when it comes early on it gives the preacher a serious problem of recovery.

Ideally the pattern of a sermon could be described as symphonic. We need movements which are crescendo and then we need diminuendo. Diminution in force and volume are important in achieving what we call an Aristotelian climax. Occasionally we find the action is in the subpoints rather than in the mains. This calls for a revision of structure so our mains will effectively carry the sermon. The question is not whether we shall attempt structure, but how we will use structural components which effectively enhance communication of the everlasting gospel.

6

What Makes a Sermon Flow?
The Issue of Fluidity

Preaching is receiving few rave reviews in our time. The interest factor is generally not high. Preaching ought to be more exciting than a ball game, but it is often as monotonous as unflavored gelatin. In one survey, preachers were asked to rank their preaching on a scale from one to ten. The preachers put their preaching at five or six on the scale, but listeners ranked them at about four and one-half. Henry Wadsworth Longfellow might well have been describing sermons when he wrote:

> Darker and darker, the black shadows fall,
> Sleep and oblivion reign over all.

The action in the church is from winkin' to blinkin' to nod. No wonder the Church of the Innerspring claims so many of our congregants.

One of the chief problems with the dull sermon is a lack of movement. The story of the bird which got into the sanctuary and flew around during the sermon is to the point. One elder was upset by the distraction, but another elder was consoling: "Thank God, something was moving!" The widespread perception that much preaching is uninteresting and dead raises the whole issue of flow and movement within content and how we can get our delivery off dead center.

We will assume that the preacher has something to say; movement is beside the point if there is no substance. Charles Haddon Spurgeon pointed out that people listen avidly to the reading of a will in court, and a man gives close attention when the judge pronounces his sentence. We must do more than piggyback on trifles, for people have lived too long on thin servings of the Word of God. Joseph Conrad said that what comes easily makes for dull reading; the same is true for preaching.

Movement within a Sermon

We must continually be prospecting for ideas to avoid elegant oversimplification, and clarifying thought through hard work in the text. Every aspect of effective preaching is hard work. As a result, sometimes it seems we live in a kind of spiritual twilight zone, so much is vague, and deep riches of God's truth are but waved to in passing. James R. Bjorge tells of a woman at beautiful Lake Louise in Alberta, Canada, who asked: "Sir, can you tell me where we can find Lake Louise?" Somewhat puzzled, the man replied: "But lady, this is Lake Louise." The woman then spun around, jumped in the car, and said to her husband: "Well, honey, we've done Lake Louise!" And off they trundled.[1] This tourist mindset sometimes carries over into our preparation for preaching.

But even the best-prepared sermon can go awry, and one reason is the pace of delivery. Some go so fast that listening to them is like drinking from a fire hydrant.

---

1. James R. Bjorge, *Forty Ways to Fortify Your Faith* (Minneapolis: Augsburg, 1984), 120.

Preaching cannot always gallop. Movement also involves the pace of covering material. There is such a thing as homiletical overkill. The more common problem is that, instead of giving a zinger, we plod along in elephantine style—voluminous and too weighty. And we often find what I call the "ferris-wheel sermon" which goes around and around but never gets anywhere. If there is minimal flow or momentum, the sermon will tend to become circular and repetitive. Few preachers never need help with the factors of flow.

Getting off the Ground

Blessed is the preacher who can get the sermon airborne without too long a runway. The takeoff or introduction is so critical to flow. The introduction is the contract for communication. If the preacher does not gain the attention of the audience in the first two or three minutes, he will probably never get it. Cicero argued that the introduction achieves three goals: It arouses interest; it secures favor; it prepares to lead. The introduction should never exceed 10 to 15 percent of the preaching time. It was said of John Owen that he often spent so much time setting the table that people lost their appetite for the sermon. There is a saying among preachers that the introduction is like a gate into an open field—and the preacher should not spend too much time swinging on it.

As Euclid wisely observed, a bad beginning means a bad ending. The preacher then needs to focus carefully on his beginning. He should not begin speaking until he is in the pulpit and has established eye contact with the listeners. The preacher should not come roaring out of the homiletical chute too fast. The introduction should be somewhat subdued, or else, where do we go from here? Gradually build momentum. There is much truth in the rhyme which calls a preacher to

> Begin low, speak slow,
> Rise higher, catch fire,
> Wax warm, sit down in a storm.

My former colleague, Lloyd M. Perry, wisely counseled that little gesture be used in the introduction. The danger of too much here is obvious, as is noted in another snippet of poetry:

> Out it streams, this panting diction,
> Carrying all things, save conviction.

H. Grady Davis quotes Gilbert Highet on the importance of the first few words of a book: they "need not be dramatic: they need not even be clear; but they must grip the mind of the reader and begin to mold his mood."[2] To begin a sermon, "The text of the morning is," is to jeopardize rapport. Fred Craddock advises preachers that they must build the nest before they lay the egg. Study the opening lines of great literary pieces. Opening lines set a confident tone, as Gertrude Stein pointed out to a young American writer who was timidly pouring tea for guests in her salon: "When you pour, young man," she thundered, "pour boldly!"[3] George Orwell plunged into *1984* by noting, "It was a bright cold day in April, and the clocks were striking 13."

Chopping up the introduction builds barriers to flow. The old German preachers used to give their introductions before their texts, but it is preferable to read the text early on, perhaps before the sermon in the order of worship or immediately upon standing to preach. A double introduction which alternates between a point of contemporary contact and contextual considerations erects an obstacle course. These elements should be carefully

2. H. Grady Davis, *Design for Preaching* (Philadelphia: Muhlenberg, 1958), 186.

3. John A. Broadus, *On the Preparation and Delivery of Sermons* (San Francisco: Harper and Row, 1979), 99.

interwoven, with some background material worked into the body of the sermon. The introduction should be as straight-line as possible, a seamless fabric in which the first transition is into the body of the message and its first main. David G. Buttrick is clear on this as he observes, "The solution to our problem is not to design a two-part introduction . . . for such an introduction would not offer a single focus to consciousness. Somehow an introduction must evoke 'a general field of meaning,' and at the same time, ready us for a first move."[4] We have seen before his warning against preannouncing the mains in the introduction. Sustain every possible suspense factor.

The strong trend in preaching today is away from backgrounding and contextual considerations which anchor us into the past, to points of contemporary contact and relevance.[5] One of the big discussions today is over inductive and deductive patterns in preaching. The inductive approach moves from the particular to the general, while in the deductive the speaker moves from general to the particular. Those who are crusading for inductive preaching, such as Fred Craddock and Ralph Lewis, tend to overstate their case. Obviously discourse needs both elements. Good thinking requires both. The anecdotal sermon never seems to eventuate in generalization, which is necessary. But concretization is equally important. As soon as an evangelical preacher has read the text, however, the basic conclusion is already set out for all. Our view of the Word in relation to preaching has settled that. In the same way an evangelical counselor can never be strictly nondirective or Rogerian—there are some givens. So the sermon needs to combine both inductive and deductive elements, but the introduction should

---

4. David G. Buttrick, *Homiletic: Moves and Structures* (Philadelphia: Fortress, 1987), 85.

5. Davis, *Design,* has an excellent discussion of relevance, beginning on 242.

be as inductive as possible, starting where the people are with significant points of contemporary contact. Further help in getting started is found in Michael J. Hostetler's fine book, *Introducing the Sermon.*[6]

Pathology in the Mains

In achieving and sustaining movement, we are looking for forms which foster momentum. I have already characterized and advanced the case for clear structure. If the sermon has so many ideas that it suffers from information overload, it will sink of its own weight. It certainly will not achieve elevation over the first treetops. Content dump is a chief mischiefmaker for the young preacher. Too much is dropped on the congregation. One of the great skills in preaching is the art of resisting the temptation to put it all in the sermon. We are drawn down appealing bypaths which do not really bear on the subject at hand. Scholarly disquisitions on the Hebrew and Greek backgrounds and darling word studies are particularly tempting. They will fascinate a few but bid adieu to most.

Some desperately seek to compensate for problems in main points with emotional gush. One of my colleagues inadvertently read a notation on a pastor's sermon outline, left on the desk in the study: "Weep here." Another pastor wrote on his manuscript: "Point weak; *shout!*" It is far better to understand the pathologies which befall mains and avoid them. Some of the common illnesses are:

1. *They are not clearly stated.* James Denney maintained that rule 1 of effective preaching is lucidity, rule 2 is lucidity, and rule 3 is lucidity.
2. *They are too obvious or too bland.* The dead air of familiarity will stifle, and the cliche can kill.

6. Michael J. Hostetler, *Introducing the Sermon: The Art of Compelling Beginnings* (Grand Rapids: Zondervan, 1986).

3. *They are not sufficiently assertive.* The main serves like a grappling hook in mountain climbing. It needs to establish an area for ascent.
4. *They are not proportionate or balanced.* The mains need to be symmetrical. A main that is malnourished by a lack of content stands out for the wrong reason.
5. *They are wrongly conceived,* as when one seeks to cover "the four horsemen of the Apocalypse" in three points.
6. *They present a premature climax.* The last main must be climactic, unless the sermon is a diamond, and each point has equal value so that the whole comprises the jewel.
7. *They misfire.* All preachers experience occasionally a main which does not ignite. This needs to be analyzed in content and form.

Trouble in the Transitions

The main points are the structural components most responsible for propelling forward progress. If we are not getting on as we should, it is to the mains we must look once we have gone beyond the introduction. If these seem sound but progress is still slow, the problem may be in our transitions. Every sermon contains transitional statements—bridges that move us into the mains, from one main to another, into and out of the subs, and into and out of illustrations and supporting materials. But sometimes the bridge washes out.

If we are "overladen with inert ideas," to use Alfred North Whitehead's trenchant phrase, not even good transitions will help us. (It has been observed that the later novels of H. G. Wells commenced well, but then sat down lumpily like a baked apple in its juice.) Subject matter and plot may well be our problem in such a sermon. There may be a stringiness which makes the texture coarse and rough. Occasionally I'll get a student who is on a veritable rampage in the sermon. The main thought has departed without the student even noticing. We can get off track so easily, and this is another reason that transitions and connectives need to be strong and effective. We would like to avoid choppiness and discontinuity.

The right illustration is invaluable. An illustration never establishes a truth—it illuminates a truth. The right story can give significant velocity to the sermon, but the wrong story or the story that doesn't exactly bear out the point at issue quickly blunts or diffuses thrust. The good illustration is driven from the inside of a point and so does not have to be coaxed or coerced into a tight fit. Too long an illustration or an illustration that must be explained will do more harm than good. It also must be true if it is represented as being so. But almost totally neglected in discussion of illustrative material is the crucial role of careful transitions into the story and out of it. These are points at which considerable thought and care must be given. I try to practice my entry and exit lines to ensure precision and effectiveness.

Books of illustrations are generally to be avoided. Spurgeon's illustrations were for another time. Today they have a dank odor of mildew and mold. Use a good mix of biblical, personal, and fresh, current illustrations. Develop a good retrieval system, ideally with a central index for your books, files, and illustrations. There is huge potential power for both your logical-thought outline and your emotional-feeling outline in good illustrations carefully and properly developed and surrounded with careful transitions.

The Movement of Words

Just as there are generative and operative sentences which expedite the development of thought, so there are words which open gates and words which close gates.

Words are more than sound and smoke. There are trigger words which can get things moving. The danger for the lover of words is to become simply a juggler of phrases. What we seek is the salty tang of freshness. Words are our stock in trade as preachers so we need to calibrate their use carefully.

Studies show that vocabulary grows dramatically during childhood, then slows down and ceases to grow at all in about the midtwenties. Since vocabulary is vital for clarity and energy in preaching, preachers should forestall this decline and remain students of words.[7] We should make words work for us, for the difference between the right word and one that is almost right is the difference between lightning and the lightning bug. The master word builder weighs jargon carefully and uses the active voice to paint pictures that show, not tell, listeners.

There are two basic approaches in building vocabulary. Wilfred J. Funk takes families of meaning, such as "verbs of violence," and "nouns of joy." This is a way to categorize words through their synonyms and antonyms.[8] Norman Lewis, on the other hand, takes the etymological approach by studying Latin and Greek roots, prefixes, and suffixes.[9] This is a fruitful approach but does not enrich us with the powerful Anglo-Saxon words. (It is interesting to note that many short, vivid, descriptive words derive from Anglo-Saxon.)

"Always read with a pen in your hand," Benjamin Franklin said. I have long kept a word notebook. Jot down the word and look it up. The preacher must be a student of connotation in words, looking beyond what a word means to what it implies. S. I. Hayakawa observes

7. James W. Cox, *Preaching* (San Francisco: Harper and Row, 1985), 220; Fred Craddock, *Preaching* (Nashville: Abingdon, 1985), 198.

8. Wilfred J. Funk, *Six Weeks to Words of Power* (New York: Funk and Wagnalls, Pocket Books, 1953).

9. Norman Lewis, *Instant Word Power* (New York: AMSCO School Publications, New American Library, 1981).

that there are "snarl" words and "purr" words. "Weasel" words say what we don't mean. "Weary" words are those worn down like pebbles; they no longer clash but simply roll with the stream. Poverty of expression and the inability to say something in a striking way hobble the preacher of our time. The English language is vast— 800,000 words, as compared to German with 185,000 or French with 100,000. The average preacher uses 50,000 words. Let's aspire to a clean and certain sound.

The Movement of Emotion

At its root, the flow of delivery is how communicative we are. Some preachers favor pulpit pyrotechnics. Others talk as if they fear they will be overheard by the FBI. What we need is a warm, outgoing personality—passion, not cold distance. We need evocatory communication. As Walter Wangerin admonishes, "Pitch it to the audience, and don't forget the children!" Thomas Guthrie said that the manner of preaching is to its matter as powder is to the ball.

This is powder and shot which are fired purposefully, or, as John Cotton advised preachers, "Let flye point blank." Every person in George Whitefield's audience felt as though the message was for him or her alone. He foamed with prophetic, personal urgency. Some preachers have so little charisma because they approach their subject with little authority. In H. G. Wells's *History* the author uses "we think" or "suppose" or "it is our opinion" 726 times. There is no place for a preacher who stutters, "Everyone outside of Christ is going to hell, I think."

I am not forgetting that a lack of vital wattage may be caused by temperamental reserve. I will not argue that an introvert cannot be an effective preacher, for a soft-spoken person can have moments of effective intensity. I'm not talking about loudness but feeling, as Richard Baxter described:

> I preached as never to preach again,
> And as a dying man to dying men.

One of the candidates for the presidency in the primaries of 1988 had a razor-sharp organization and some good stunts, but his public appearances were a debacle. It was observed that what he lacked was the ability to "reduce complex issues to simple evocative images that can capture a mass audience and inspire it."[10] Donald M. Macleod quotes David H. C. Read's definition of charisma as "an elusive quality of charm, personal magnetism and personal power, the capacity to excite one's fellowmen."[11] If this definition discourages you because you feel you have the personality of a slug, Macleod reminds us that we are talking here about spiritual dynamics. Aspects of this will be discussed in subsequent chapters on creativity and the use of imagination. But beyond question there is a warmth and passion required in this spiritual ice age, what Jonathan Edwards described as a "fixed engagedness of the heart."

T. Harwood Pattison gives us this word picture of John Chrysostom, the "golden-mouthed" preacher of Constantinople:

> As he advanced from exposition to practical appeals, his delivery became gradually more rapid, his countenance more animated, his voice more vivid and intense. The people began to hold in their breath. The joints of their loins were loosed. A creeping sensation like that produced by a series of electric waves passed over them. They felt as if drawn toward the pulpit by a sort of magnetic influence . . . some rose from their seats, others were overcome by a kind of faintness and the great mass could only hold their heads and give vent to their emotions in tears.

10. Dan Goodgame, "Standing Up for Substance," *Time* 131 (January 4, 1988): 44.

11. Donald M. Macleod, *The Problem of Preaching* (Philadelphia: Fortress, 1987), 85.

Natural gift? The power of the Spirit? It is certainly both. I can only pray with John Calvin as he was wont in ascending into his pulpit in Geneva, "Come, Holy Spirit, come."

7

How Can We Escape Predictability?
The Issue of Variety

Look back over your sermons of the last month. Are there some persistent patterns? Are we in a groove which could soon become our grave? One of the curses of the contemporary pulpit is its total predictability. This is lethal.

"When you preach, you do not know what you do: you wield lightning!" said Auguste Lecerf. Or do we? Old motor mouth holds forth in his Gothic ghetto facing seas of empty seats. Eleven o'clock and all is well. The preacher trained in his education factory seems impervious in his homiletical tortoise shell. The preacher and the congregation are narcotized by the weekly "drip, drip, drip" of the status quo. Thomas Carlyle condemned the endless chopping of straw in the pulpit.

Going to church ought to be like approaching a volcano. Our churches are full of anniversary Christians whose chief preoccupation is the commemoration of events in the past. These Christians are going nowhere. They are deaf to the music of heaven. The corridors of their minds are undisturbed. Their favorite Bible verse seems to be "I shall not be moved," or possibly, "My heart is fixed." They seem to wear invisible earmuffs so that preaching does not make much dent.

No small part of the banality of such a Christianity is the preaching of intellectual sharecroppers whose sermons are irksome prattle, basically Saturday-night specials. So poorly prepared, no wonder the homiletical loaf is half-baked. The old Irish cook began a recipe for Irish stew: "First catch the rabbit." There must be something of substance to share or the sermon will be just so much psychobabble about the latest fad. How shall we get our hearers to change their headsets? One way is to be less tedious in preaching. The preacher needs to be "lively, supple and always at the window," like England's prime minister, William E. Gladstone (1809–1898), of whom it was said: "He always keeps himself on the line of discovery."

What makes dull preaching so inexcusable is that God's Word is extraordinarily interesting. Scripture itself has incredible variety. Just as God's works in creation show vast diversity, so God's Word in revelation displays an inexhaustible array of succulent passages. God loves variety and so should we. One person boasted, "Our preacher can preach twelve different sermons from one text," to which his friend countered: "Our preacher can take any text and preach the same sermon."

The preacher today needs to be constantly on the prowl for new ways of sharing the "old, old story" which is ever new. Stephen Olford says that no two messages should be the same in any sequence of four sermons. We need the willingness to look at what we are doing and to be open to some change. In so doing we recognize the danger in any innovation to call attention to itself.[1] This would be self-defeating. We also must beware of irreverence or the tasteless. How shall we achieve the goal in our preaching of variety within the bounds of propriety?

1. C. S. Lewis, *Letters to Malcolm: Chiefly on Prayer* (New York: Harcourt, Brace, and World, 1964), 4.

Variety Through Selection and the Preaching Plan

Random selection of texts and topics will be prone to sameness. As we systematically and thoroughly preach the whole counsel of God, we shall be more apt to reflect the Grand Canyon glories of Holy Scripture. Charles Haddon Spurgeon commented, "Give me the Bible and the Holy Ghost and I can go on preaching forever." We seem to know more and more about less and less. Soon we shall know everything about nothing, or so it seems.

So modern preaching has often become less systematic and skips over the blinding and appalling enormities of divine revelation to deal with nitpicking trivialities. Who cares that Harcatius, King of Persia centuries ago, was a notable mole catcher? Someone must suffer for the sermon. If it is not the preacher who is willing to pay the price then it will be the congregation.

Preparation that results in variety in selection is hard work. There is something in preaching of trying to pump water uphill. Preparation is of two kinds: indirect, the studying and reading we do over the years, and direct, what we do for a specific message. If we torture ourselves weekly with the question, "What am I going to preach?" we shall be too susceptible to predictable and familiar paths. We need a plan. The plan may be an expository book series blended with biographical, doctrinal, and issue series, or it may be preaching the church year, or a combination of these. I used a two- and a three-year plan to ensure that, with three or four preparations weekly, I would not get into imbalance. I need to stake out both Old and New Testaments, both Gospel and epistolary, both panoramic and microscopic perspectives. To preach Philippians in the morning and 1 John in the evening would be a mistake. We need to balance the more didactic with a narrative series in the evening. George Morrison of the Wellington Church, Glasgow, Scotland, followed an expository course in the morning and then something of wider scope in the evenings.

Andrew W. Blackwood, in his now dated but still apropos *Planning a Year's Pulpit Work,* makes an effective case for seasonal objectives:

September to Christmas—undergirding

Christmas to Easter—recruiting

Easter to Pentecost—instructing

Pentecost to September—heartening[2]

Although Christmas and Easter are the high points of the church year and celebrative occasions of the highest order, I have always found these the hardest times to preach because so much has been said on their subjects. O for a fresh and zestful word! It is well to lay out one's Easter sermons over the years—if we have been preaching preponderantly from the Gospel record, perhaps we should turn to Acts or Revelation 1 or even an Old Testament text for a change.

The philosophy of "if you must plan, plan after" is a pathetic abdication of responsibility. Pastoral preaching of funerals and wedding homilies is an urgent case. Do we always say about the same thing? Develop a funeral notebook where verses and thoughts can be planted like seedlings to sprout and germinate, and then be transplanted into the specific situation of need.

Planning ahead avoids always going to the barrel. Every preacher, even more itinerant servants of Christ, need the discipline of fresh preparation on a regular basis. Seminary professors and denominational executives can go stale by perpetual repetition of previously used materials.

2. Andrew W. Blackwood, *Planning a Year's Pulpit Work* (New York: Abingdon-Cokesbury, 1942), 19.

In one parish, I recognized that my predecessor had given superb exposition in depth for twenty-five years. For a change of pace for the congregation and myself, we initiated a five-year Bible reading program, reading Genesis then Matthew, Exodus then Mark, until we had read the Old Testament once and the New Testament twice in five years. The messages were drawn from the reading portions of the week. A daily five-minute radio broadcast highlighted a practical application of the day's reading and came on just after noon so many factory workers could listen during their lunch hour. It was an excellent tonic for my own soul.

Any series needs to be subject to interruption. A national crisis or local issue may require the insertion of a timely message to help our people interpret the situation within a biblical frame of reference. The four Sundays of Advent leading up to Christmas afford even the less liturgical an opportunity to deepen understanding of Christ's incarnation. I am about as liturgical as a corn cob, but I increasingly value the Lenten season as an opportunity for something special on the cross. It baffles me that so few evangelicals mark Pentecost Sunday or Whitsuntide, the day we remember the outpouring of the Holy Spirit. Indeed, if Mother's Day and Pentecost coincide, the Holy Spirit doesn't have a chance. How many preachers have never shared on the ascension of our Lord? Mariano di Gangi has given us an excellent sample of preaching the church year[3] and my colleague Richard A. Bodey has edited a recent volume of suggestive sermons which can prime this pump.[4]

Biographical preaching is frequently a good break after a heavier course, and one should not neglect doctrinal preaching in which we seek to bring together great

3. Mariano di Gangi, *Word for All Seasons: Preaching Through the Christian Year* (Grand Rapids: Baker, 1980).
4. Richard A. Bodey, ed., *Good News for All Seasons* (Grand Rapids: Baker, 1986).

texts which treat of the mountainous themes of our faith. Phillips Brooks scored the point well when he advised us to "Preach doctrine, preach all the doctrine you know, and learn forever more and more; but preach it always, not that men may believe it, but that men may be saved by believing it."[5] Eschatology, although sometimes overdone, is a most relevant and practical focus for the articulation of the Christian hope. It is a good counterpoint for the evening service. In some areas the evening service is in tough shape. We may be moving toward the time when certain magnet churches in given geographical areas will have the evening service, but the answer is not the shallow and the ephemeral but the solid and the substantial. In any event, careful and prayerful planning with good advance time for reflection and creative brooding will allow us to take long strides toward greater variety in our preaching.

Creative Use of the Components

Our foundational premise rules out gimmicks and stunts. James Denney argues that no one can preach Christ and be clever at the same time. I am aghast to read of a preacher who feels that the pulpit is so passé that in lieu of the sermon he reads newspaper clippings and divides his congregation into buzz groups to discuss the issue. We must stay with the Book!

But we also need to reflect honestly about the ruts into which we have fallen. For one thing we can vary the size of the preaching text. One of the most personally rewarding Sunday evening series I ever preached was on "The Prophets Speak to Our Times." I encapsulated the essential message of each Old Testament prophet into a single message, such as "Amos Speaks to Our Affluence" and "Jonah Speaks to Our Persistent Prejudice." Sometimes

5. Phillips Brooks, *Lectures on Preaching* (New York: E. P. Dutton, 1877; reprint ed., Grand Rapids: Zondervan, 1950), 129.

we should take a whole book, a whole chapter, a whole paragraph, or simply a single verse, giving careful attention to context in every case. There are alternating currents here which will make for effective variety. We need to be spiritual sleuths searching out nuggets in an endless thrill of discovery. Lloyd M. Perry and Faris D. Whitesell in their now out-of-print but worthwhile volume, *Variety in Your Preaching,* show something of the full range of variation possible in the use of our components.[6]

Another enlivening aid is to vary the pattern of entry into the sermon. A probing question, a pungent quotation, a moving description, or a brief illustration are but a few of the variant possibilities. Using a different number of main points is important. Break the triadic pattern. Shock your congregation with a good two-point message (problem/solution) or use no formal points at all in preaching a narrative sermon. The uniqueness of the narrative sermon is a subject of lively import with today's interest in "telling the story," and some preachers have neglected narrative sections of Scripture to the great impoverishment of their flocks. Bruce Waltke figures 75 percent of the Old Testament is narrative. What an explosive element for contemporary preaching.

Illustrations need to be a mixed grill. We must neither overuse nor underuse personal illustrations. Some congregations overdose on sports stories. Sports addicts need to remember that some people can't stand Monday night football. Or some congregations get a steady diet of stories about the dog or the kids. My children very early on made me promise not to use them for illustrations. They did everyone a great favor. How carefully we must use case studies in various difficulties lest we terminate all counseling opportunities. Even to use some cases anonymously should involve obtaining permission. Members of a former charge may be visiting when we

6. Lloyd M. Perry and Faris D. Whitesell, *Variety in Your Preaching* (Westwood, N.J.: Revell, 1954).

think we are safe in using dated materials. Much attention needs to be paid to variation in the conclusion. Here is where the predictable recapitulation becomes an invitation to inattention.

The skilled composer in the development of the theme will introduce a diminished seventh chord which enables a shift to a new and very different key. We need new and unexpected directions in sermons to face the fact that people know what we're going to say before we open our mouths. Since our message is a given from Scripture, we evangelical/fundamental preachers must give all the more attention to creative and imaginative use of structure and form.

We need to cultivate stylistic variation. Many of us are labored and ponderous in style. We need the wise use of humor to liven it up.[7] John Calvin advocated that the sermon should be lively. This means we must preach suggestively, not exhaustively. We do not generally have as long a time to preach as was formerly the case. While not capitulating to what P. T. Forsythe called the "fatal urgency for brevity," we must leave the audience wanting more. This is the day when the ten-minute oil change is too slow; the automatic teller is too slow; the microwave is too slow. We need to consciously vary pace, pitch, volume, and punch in our delivery. No matter how rich our content may be, if we steadily gaze at the back window we have severely constricted preaching effectiveness with predictable delivery patterns.

Innovative Forms and Techniques

How venturesome and experimental dare we be? An unusually fine contribution at this point is the book by Harold Freeman on *Variety in Biblical Preaching*.[8] Here

7. John W. Drakeford, *Humor in Preaching* (Grand Rapids: Ministry Resources Library, 1986).

8. Harold Freeman, *Variety in Biblical Preaching* (Waco: Word, 1987).

is a good case for the use of some variant forms, but to
some degree innovation must fit the personality of the
preacher. This whole area is something of a mine field,
but we can scarce afford to be oblivious to some new
possibilities for occasional use. In employing a form for
the first time, it would be wise to prepare the way—
perhaps use it at the evening service or another occasional service first. Invite comment and suggestion.
Build a climate and an atmosphere in which some risk
can be taken, and there can even be mistakes and room
to grow and develop. Does it always have to be perfect?
These are real issues when we face new forms.

Freeman is not proposing that innovation replace the
traditional but that it augment and enhance the traditional. An example is the dramatic monologue or "first-
person" sermon. In teaching on variety in preaching I
generally set out two rounds of preaching. In the first
round we press for the use of variety in structure and
components in either didactic or narrative passages. In
the second round we require either a "first-person" or a
dialogue sermon. For many students without any background in drama or oral interpretation, this is totally
new ground. Possibilities for variation are infinite. Some
costume for the character. Others will use partial costume or some props and visuals. Some will represent one
character such as Achan in Joshua 7 through the whole
message. One student gave us the Book of Ruth in three
parts: Naomi, then Boaz, and finally Joseph out of
Matthew 1, reflecting on his decision regarding Mary and
whether he should act in accord with the principle of
hesed-kindness as had Boaz, his forebear. Some will play
the role for a time and then move out of character to a
final segment of interpretation and application. This
necessitates a decision as to whether we shall have indirect or direct application. This also raises the complex
issue of transition.

The danger in the thoughtful and careful development

of the biblical situation is that we may leave it "back there, embalmed in history." The most satisfying experience I have had along these lines is the presentation of the action of the Book of Philemon as Philemon, Apphia, and Archippus see Onesimus, the runaway slave, returning to their estate in the Lycus Valley. Onesimus brings a scroll from the apostle Paul. I then, as Philemon, read the letter amid comments and observations. The format brings out the significance and spiritual impact of this remarkable example of Christian courtesy.

Several preachers of my acquaintance have used a "first person" for Easter Sunday morning to elicit considerable interest and attention in the larger community. One has used costume and another has not. The question as to which character would be used in a given year has increased interest. One of my doctor of ministry students has developed such expertise that he uses the dramatic form with regularity and is in demand in this country and abroad as an effective communicator.

The dialogue sermon is a form requiring two fairly well-matched individuals who interact side by side. Many diverse formats are possible. Some years ago my brother and I did a dialogue sermon entitled "Christian Certainty in Modern Perplexity." The whole area of increasing dialogical profile in preaching is important for us. Where the worship service precedes the Sunday school hour, dialogue can lead to profitable discussion of the sermon in the class. I have frequently used a sermon discussion after a Sunday evening service. When we are in a provocative series—"The Ten Commandments and Today's Crises" or some issue-oriented series—we'll adjourn to the fellowship hall with coffee and doughnuts and open up the mike. The aim of dialogue is to counter detachment and the spectator syndrome which have so grievously afflicted many churches.

There are limitless ways to enhance preaching through various media. Constant use of the overhead can

turn the sanctuary into a lecture-hall and pose difficulties for those who have visual problems. Anything we do
all the time will lose its effectiveness. The use of artifacts
and visuals in preaching must be done carefully and with
good planning and integration. I've used a facsimile of
one of the nails used to crucify Jesus and some thorn
stock from Gethsemane. One gifted preacher used five or
six slides at the beginning of each exposition on the seven
churches of Asia Minor. This entails planning and work!

While H. Marshall McLuhan was correct in arguing
that "the spoken word involves all of the senses dramatically,"[9] we need to recognize that people respond in different ways emotionally, or in what researchers call
"modalities." A former Th.M. student, Toby Sorrels,
applied these modalities to the preaching situation in a
major research paper. He observes that there are persons
who are definitely more visual; television really appeals
to them. They will say, "I see what you are saying." Other
people are more auditory: "I hear what you're saying,"
they respond. These persons are in a kind of running
internal dialogue with themselves. Still other people are
more kinesthetic and will say "I'm in touch" or "I don't
feel." To communicate to a group of divergent people the
preacher should want to make contact with all three
modalities. This whole area needs much more research
and exploration in relation to the preaching and communication opportunities in our times.

No one of us is excused from the anguish and hard
work of seeking more effective variety in preaching.
Thomas Babington Macaulay said of Lord Henri Galway
at the Battle of Almanza, fought in 1707: "He thought it
more honorable to fail according to the rules than to succeed by innovation." How desirous are we of really communicating? I like what Bishop Joseph Yeakel prays as
he begins every sermon: "And now, O God, either through
me or in spite of me, speak to your people." May it be so.

9. Ibid., 52.

8

Why Is Application So Difficult?
The Issue of Relevancy

As Bessie Brooks and Tommy Snooks
Walked out of church on Sunday,
Said Bessie Brooks to Tommy Snooks:
"Tomorrow will be Monday!"

I've heard Haddon Robinson quote that ditty several times, and it epitomizes one of the preacher's continuing and nagging issues. The preacher must be concerned to bridge the worlds of the truth of God's Word and the realities of people's lives. Harold Freeman uses the analogy of welding with "the preaching arc" to fuse biblical revelation and the current situation.[1] J. Randall Nichols correctly asserts that people do not have a burning desire to hear what happened to the Jebusites. As the text is read, members of the congregation may, as Merrill Abbey supposes, be wondering: "What do a bunch of camel drivers have to say to me in the jet age?" The purpose of preaching reaches beyond the accurate exposition of the biblical text. The sermon which starts in the Bible and stays in the Bible is not biblical.

1. Harold Freeman, *Variety in Biblical Preaching* (Waco: Word, 1987), 28.

It can plausibly be argued that one of the key differences between preaching and teaching is that preaching is application. Indeed, John A. Broadus asserts that application in a sermon "is not merely an appendage to the discussion or a subordinate part of it, but is the main thing to be done."[2] He quotes Daniel Webster: "When a man preaches to me, I want him to make it a personal matter, a personal matter, a personal matter!"[3] Application is not an add-on. It draws from the text a meaning for life as it is being lived.

"All Scripture is God-breathed and profitable" (2 Tim. 3:16–17). The Bible is relevant to individual and corporate life and experience at all levels. It is in the very nature of God's profitable truth that it must be applied. D. Martyn Lloyd-Jones, in his careful exposition of Ephesians, insists that "truth must always be applied . . . a true understanding of the truth always does lead to application. So that if a man does not apply the truth, his real trouble is that he has not understood it."[4]

We state the truth—"So what?" the hearers legitimately demand. Call it concretion or amplification or contextualization or "uses" as did the Puritans, we are wrestling with an integral part of authentic biblical preaching. Exposition without application is like a banquet without silverware. They are to be intertwined. Yet we often shoot over the heads of our listeners by misuse of words, and we miss with off-target applications. Application is difficult.

There always exists some tension between theory and practice. The Bible student's great love for the truth of the Scripture easily leads to valuing the truth simply because it is truth. Knowledge can become a useful orna-

2. John A. Broadus, *On the Preparation and Delivery of Sermons* (San Francisco: Harper and Row, 1979), 165.

3. Ibid.

4. D. Martyn Lloyd-Jones, *Darkness and Light: An Exposition of Ephesians 4:17–5:17* (Grand Rapids: Baker, 1982), 200–201.

ment. Yet Søren Kierkegaard was right when he said: "There is no lack of information . . . something else is lacking." We must beware of the purely cognitive. Novelist Saul Bellow's words could aptly characterize much preaching in our time: "For feeling or response, they substitute acts of comprehension."[5] But abstractness is always a great enemy of preaching. The sermon is an invitation. It is a knock on the door. It is not only to inform; it must inflame.

Sometimes we are hesitant to apply because we fear repercussions. We may keep some parishioners happy if we preach only the generalities. This attitude is expressed by Lord Melbourne, Queen Victoria's first prime minister, who lamented, "Things are coming to a pretty pass if religion is going to start being personal."[6] As long as a preacher intones the general principle of the eighth commandment all is placid; when he moves to preaching against stealing logs from the company pond he is in serious trouble.

Sometimes we are afraid to apply because we feel deficient in our own experience. Not only must we find the text, but also we must let the text find us, sustaining this confidence that what has spoken to our heart will speak to others. So difficult is application that some of us veer toward G. Campbell Morgan's position that it is the Holy Spirit who must make the application. Yet what is our part to be?

The Prerequisites for Application

If the text is going to be applied properly it must be dealt with carefully. We must do more than wallow in content for, as John Henry Newman observed, definite-

5. Quoted in Ronald E. Sleeth, *God's Word and Our Words: Basic Homiletics* (Atlanta: John Knox, 1986), 69.
6. Quoted in D. Martyn Lloyd-Jones, *The Christian Warfare* (Grand Rapids: Baker, 1976), 157.

ness is vital: "Nothing is so fatal to the effect of the sermon as the habit of preaching two or three subjects at once." Newman added that little comes from a discourse on the general subject of virtue. The preacher "must aim at imprinting on the heart what will never leave it, and this he cannot do unless he employs himself on some definite object."[7] Effective application results from a clear correspondence between the text and the situation. The five stones which David used to kill Goliath can hardly be used to sum up the five principles of teaching homiletics in a seminary. This would be to disregard what the stones represent.

The text of Scripture is not merely an opening quotation. Like Jacob said to his challenger, the preacher must say to his text: "Unless you bless me, I will not let you go." We must ask the hard questions of the text: Is this descriptive or prescriptive? Is it properly illustrative? Our instinct for relevance must foster a great solicitude for the text we want to apply. We must be stethoscopic. We must listen to that text. In the interest of preaching "a right meaty Gospel," we need first to sink our teeth into the text.

Powerful application also requires that we know our people. Sometimes our failure as preachers is that we fail as pastors. Notice the pastoral context of Paul's one sermon in Acts to an audience of believers (Acts 20:13–38). The personal touch is needed, more than just foyer friendliness. "Whom you would change, you must first love," it has been maintained. Skilled application rises out of a shepherd's sensitive and loving awareness of the sheep. Do we sense the wistful stare of men and women in need? How piercing are the sorrows of this world, how painful the stigma of nobodiness to our consciousness. There is such a great cavity in the human spirit without the sense of God.

7. John Henry Newman, *The Idea of a University, Defined and Illustrated* (London: Longmans, Green and Co., 1886), 411.

Of course there will be customer resistance. Martin Luther said that when we preach the truth the dogs will begin to bark. He advised Philip Melanchthon, "Preach so that if the people don't hate their sin, they will hate you." But Lloyd-Jones wisely warns of expecting too much of the people, putting the rack too high so they can't reach the hay.[8] We must be wary of too much Tabasco. One preacher was described as angry and scolding, a cross between Attila the Hun and a snapping turtle. The needed truth and its necessary application will not always be perceived as such by our auditors. Sometimes we address a question no one is asking because it is a question which needs to be asked. There are times when pressing concerns about the future don't appeal to folk who are more interested in where they have come from than in where they are going. David G. Buttrick calls for preaching on long-range issues which may not seem immediately relevant but which dare to envision the future.[9]

Both careful foundational work in the text and sensitive knowledge of the people are requisite for effective application.

The Parameters of Application

Application begins in the introduction. Significant points of contemporary and personal contact initially in communication dig solid footings for subsequent bridging. Traditionally the American application has been given in the conclusion while the British have tended toward continuous application. In most cases (except for a ladder or a seek-and-find or interrogative outline), the continuous application is much to be preferred. There is

8. Iain H. Murray, *David Martyn Lloyd-Jones: The First Forty Years, 1899–1939* (Carlisle, Pa.: Banner of Truth, 1981), 183.

9. David G. Buttrick, *Homiletic: Moves and Structures* (Philadelphia: Fortress, 1987), 328.

a risk in leaving the application in one chunk at the end. If it is missed there, the impact is zero. It may seem more like addendum if it is totally deferred, like a commercial at the end of the program which can easily be dismissed. If it is organismically interwoven in the fabric of the developing message, it creeps upon us somewhat unawares.

Should application be direct or indirect? Direct application spells out in specific ways precisely what the implementation of the principle should entail. There is a place for direct application, but it surrenders all subtlety. The danger is to be perceived as talking down to a congregation, patronizing them by belaboring the obvious. It is possible to explain too much. A little girl said to her well-intentioned mother, "I think I could understand it if you didn't explain it." The indirect application is always suggestive, not exhaustive. The preacher is more a prompter than the oracle of all wisdom. Fred Craddock has advocated what he calls "overhearing the Gospel." This in light of the alleged fact that "individuals are becoming more and more reluctant to accept explicit application, religious or otherwise, to their daily lives. That kind of prescription implies that one person is in a position to tell others just what they should do with their daily lives."[10] In a fine discussion, J. Daniel Baumann lists four different kinds of indirect application which give a spacious and roomy sense: illustration, multiple options, narration, and testimony.[11] In this way the preacher throws the ball into the hands of the hearers and says, "You take it. It's yours now."

We need both direct and indirect application. "You are the man!" Nathan cried to King David in 2 Samuel 12:17. The blending of both in continuous application seems

10. Carl E. Larson, "Factors in Small Group Interaction," *Preaching* (November-December 1968): 19.

11. J. Daniel Baumann, *An Introduction to Contemporary Preaching* (Grand Rapids: Baker, 1972), 250–51.

advantageous. To always leave application at the level of the generic is to sidestep duty. The danger of specificity is in the narrowing of focus. If we cite one specific sin, then those not guilty of that infraction feel off the hook. To use the case study or the paradigm approach opens doors for application. There should be a clear feel that the preacher is not speaking to the congregation generally but to the persons within the assembly. Many cues and signals of a vocal and nonvocal nature can reinforce the impression that we are being addressed as persons. The "life-situation" preaching of the generation just past generally addressed felt needs and aches, but frequently it was without clear scriptural principalization. The main thought of the text should be the main thought of the application.[12]

This is what the preacher uniquely offers from Scripture. As Reinhold Niebuhr said, "Without an adequate sermon, no clue is given to the moral purpose at the heart of the mystery, and reverence remains without ethical content."

The Patterns of Application

The impression of great difficulty in application is corroborated by the almost total lack of significant monographs or volumes on the subject. Several doctoral students for whom I am mentor are working in this area and confirm the paucity of material. Most generally seminary training is not helpful at this point. Our dean at Trinity Evangelical Divinity School, Walter C. Kaiser, Jr., speaks to this point:

A gap of crisis proportions exists between the steps generally outlined in most seminary or Biblical training classes in exegesis and the hard realities most pastors

12. Walter C. Kaiser, Jr., *Toward an Exegetical Theology* (Grand Rapids: Baker, 1981), 18.

face every week as they prepare their sermons. Nowhere
in the total curriculum of theological studies has the student been more deserted and left to his own devices than
in bridging the yawning chasm between understanding
the content of Scripture as it was given in the past and
proclaiming it with such relevance in the present as to
produce faith, life and bona fide works.[13]

Many a sermon leaves us motivated to do something,
whether serve or witness or hope or rejoice, but we are
abandoned on the ropes because the "how-to" step is
missing. Early on in ministry I was arrested by the
anguished remorse of a dedicated layperson who said,
"Pastor, I have longed to win a soul to Christ but after
all of these years I have never won anyone to the Savior.
No one has ever taught me how." If teaching is chiefly a
subject to be inculcated, preaching is chiefly an object to
be achieved in the everyday world. A secular communications expert says, "When we learn to phrase our purposes in terms of specific responses from those attending
our messages, we have taken the first step towards effi-
cient and effective communication."[14] The sermon must
be as concrete as a sidewalk in this sense.

J. I. Packer has called our attention to the thinking
and practice of the Puritans with respect to the preaching of the Word.[15] This is embodied in their volume, *The
Westminster Directory for the Publick Worship of God.*
Referring to this duty of the preacher it says:

> He is not to rest in general doctrine, although ever so
> much cleared and confirmed, but to bring it home by spe-
> cial use, by application to his hearers: which albeit prove
> a work of great difficulty to himself, requiring much pru-

13. Ibid.
14. David K. Berlo, *The Process of Communication: An Introduction to
Theory and Practice* (New York: Holt, Rinehart and Winston, 1960).
15. I am indebted to my colleague, Richard Allen Bodey, for these notes
from a class taught by J. I. Packer at Trinity Evangelical Divinity School,
Deerfield, Ill., Spring 1988.

dence, zeal and meditation, and to the natural and corrupt man will be very unpleasant; yet he is to endeavor to perform it in such a manner, that his auditors may feel the word of God to be quick and powerful, and a discerner of the thoughts and intents of the heart; and that, if any unbeliever or ignorant person be present, he may have the secrets of his heart made manifest, and give glory to God.[16]

Packer has prepared an application grid such as was employed by Puritan preachers, in which he identifies five objects of application:

1. informing the mind of truth to be understood and falsehood to be eschewed
2. impacting the will of duties to be undertaken and the means to be employed
3. igniting the affections to show the miseries and dangers of sin together with the remedies and the best ways to avoid them
4. applying comfort, giving encouragement, whether general or particular, and carefully answering such questions as the troubled heart and afflicted spirit may suggest to the contrary
5. initiating self-examination for those in trial[17]

Each of these objects should be weighed in relation to certain kinds of hearers: those asleep, seekers, young, old, fallen, and sad. Objects and types of hearers are not to be sought from every text in every sermon, but something of a spread and comprehensiveness should be attempted over a period of preaching. Such "uses" are to be selected "as, by his residence and conversing with his flock, he findeth most needful and seasonable; and, amongst these, such as may most draw their souls to

16. *The Confession of Faith* (Edinburgh: Johnstone, Hunter and Co., 1884), 292.
17. Packer, class notes.

Christ, the fountain of light, holiness and comfort." Such a grid and thoughtful plan could prove most useful in any pastor's quest for effective application.

The Problems of Application

Any preacher who pursues Scripture systematically and who hears the cry of the listeners to "tell us what the good news is," will preach the *kerygma,* that is, evangelistic messages. To preach only evangelistic messages would be to starve the people of God. Yet never to preach a gospel message and invite sinners to receive Christ is to fail to proclaim the whole counsel of God. Evangelistic preaching should be especially doctrinal and often more apologetical. Building bridges to the secular mind is a special challenge, part of what Frederick W. Robertson called "the intense excitement of preaching." Some have special gifts in preaching to the unconverted, but all pastors in "doing the work of an evangelist" need to hone skills which can make the evangelistic application with finesse and force. Nor should we be surprised to discover that there may be regular, long-time attendees who have never been born again.

No genre is as plagued with histrionics as is evangelistic preaching. The current political arena, with its feeling that issue folks are about as welcome as ants at a picnic, is analogous to current evangelism's focus on personality instead of principle. Messages go out in three-word sound bites. There is no possibility of brain-sprain because so many evangelists seem to be resting their brains while preaching.

Although certain messages are avowedly evangelistic in purpose, it remains possible without twisting meaning or obstructing flow to share enough of Jesus Christ in every message so an unconverted person could have enough to be saved. It is no imposition on the biblical message to refer clearly and compellingly to the Lord

Jesus with whom we may have a living personal relationship through faith in his all-sufficient sacrifice for sin. Some superb materials are available to help us with the evangelistic application and the giving of the public invitation in various contexts.[18]

The concern for relevancy and practical application exposes us unconsciously to the peril of becoming too hortatory. Some preachers are really exhorters. This seemed a special calling of the late Vance Havner, who was an itinerant through most of his ministry. But the resident pastor must beware continually laying out burdens too heavy to be carried. There are a lot of broken hearts out there, so preaching should not be an ordeal service after service. Such preaching tends toward thin moralism, an endless mass of dos and don'ts. I remember a motor garage in Minneapolis which carried the invitation: "Limp in, leap out." Isn't this a delightful description of what ought to be a regular experience of our people as they come to worship?

While our goals and aims are high as they reflect Christ's great expectation of us, we must beware in application of setting the goal so high we actually discourage ardor. Jesus said, "My yoke is easy" (Matt. 11:30), and 1 John 5:3 adds, "His commands are not burdensome." James inveighed at the Jerusalem council that "it is my judgment, therefore, that we should not make it difficult for the Gentiles who are turning to God" (Acts 15:19). Notice also in the missive sent from the council, "It seemed good to the Holy Spirit and to us not to burden you with anything beyond the following . . ." (Acts 15:28). Our reach will exceed our grasp.

Even our divine Lord told his disciples, "I have much more to say to you, more than you can now bear" (John

18. These include D. Martyn Lloyd-Jones, *Evangelistic Sermons at Aberavon* (Carlisle, Pa.: Banner of Truth, 1983); R. Alan Street, *The Effective Invitation* (New York: Revell, 1984); R. T. Kendall, *Stand Up and Be Counted* (Grand Rapids: Zondervan, 1985).

16:12). While we face, on the one hand, the danger of diluting New Testament norms into a theology of the feasible, we must also watch in making application to a heterogeneous audience that our goals are specific, measurable, concrete, and attainable. I recall vividly from some experiments in my undergraduate studies what were called goal discrepancy factors. It is demonstrable that one can set the goals so high that they become counterproductive and discouraging, just as in setting them too low one sacrifices any motivational value in goal-setting at all. It is a wise and sensitive teacher or preacher who sets the goals high enough to summon the individual to a real run at it, but not so utterly beyond reach that the runner feels hopeless.

There is no easy or quick route to effective application in preaching. The process demands much thought and prayer. It helps if the hearers sense that their preacher is also in the process of pilgrimage toward the prize. As an American preacher once perceptively pointed out, it was not Elisha's staff, placed by his servant on the face of the dead child, that effected the miracle. It was the power of God through the personal touch.

9

How Can We Be More Imaginative in Our Preaching?
The Issue of Creativity

More imagination and creativity in preaching is one of the featured topics in almost every clinic or conference on preaching today. Preaching is an intensely creative event. This is not to say that we "make up" the sermon. We've got to be clear that the Bible is our source. Elizabeth Achtemeier reports that the Christian pulpit is suffering from nonbiblical and even heretical preaching. She points, for example, to a California clergyman who said to her, "I believe that we are all incarnations of God." Achtemeier said such clergy preach nonbiblical sermons, "not only because they do not know what the Bible says and how to study it, but also because they do not understand the most basic theology of the Christian Church."[1] In such a void creativity would be calamitous.

But given the richness of biblical revelation, we must insist that preaching is both "theology and art," as Achtemeier maintains. The preacher is not simply a techni-

---

1. Elizabeth Achtemeier, *Preaching as Theology and Art* (Nashville: Abingdon, 1984).

cian, but a craftsman and an artist in the handling, ordering, and expressing of God's truth. The passage must govern the sermon, to be sure, but if our people are listening like a lump of dough, whose fault is it? Loyalty to the totality of biblical Christianity is no excuse for great meaningless sentences which unwind like gold-plated spaghetti. James M. Wall bemoans the blandness in the American pulpit and observes that "our church discourse is dull because we have too often adopted the rational modes of the secular without retaining its poetic aspects."[2] This is why Henry Ward Beecher went so far as to say that "the first element on which your preaching will largely depend for power and success, you will perhaps be surprised to learn, is imagination, which I regard as the most important of all elements that go to make the preacher." There is a numbing and nauseating creative malaise in much preaching which seems to compress a minimum of ideas into a maximum of words.

In one sense creativity is doing what other people don't. There are those so adept at creative expression that they can preach about Noah's ark and their listeners can hear it rain! This is bringing something new into being. Pablo Picasso said his goal was "to draw the mind in a direction it's not used to and wake it up!" For a preacher to achieve Picasso-like impact the goal must be to know and experience the text. The facts of the text are analogous to the botany of a flower. But we want more than the botany; we want the fragrance as well!

Long ago Aristotle maintained that the soul never thinks without pictures. People today are even more taken with images than with ideas. We have too much argument—discourse stripped of its mystery—in our sermons and not enough drama. Violin music has been described as the scraping of horses' tails over cats' bowels. That definition has literal truthfulness, but it does

2. James M. Wall, "Beyond Blandness in Preaching," *Christian Century* 105 (May 11, 1988): 467.

scant justice to a violin concerto. For models of creative minds rich in images and metaphors consider our Lord and the biblical writers. W. MacNeille Dixon argued that "the mind of man is more like a picture gallery than a debating chamber."[3] But many a preacher says, "I have as much imagination as a warthog." Can anything be done about it?

The Dynamics of Creativity

Many evangelical preachers are image-poor since pictorializing is strange to those who deal with abstract truths. Yet I desperately want not only to state the truth but also to communicate it. Imagination is an aspect of creativity. Imagination nurtures impulses, flashes of insight and excitement over ideas; creativity is the result. In imagination we explode with ideas for a novel; in creativity these ideas result in the novel. To be genuinely creative, one must imagine. Frederick Buechner, one of the most contagiously creative people of our time, makes the point that imagination is the conjuring up inside one, by use of a very specific intellectual muscle, that which is absent or elusive, by making it concrete.

When we have excavated our text, we know what needs to be said, but we now face the quandary of how we shall say it for maximum clarity and memorability. At all costs we want to avoid the prefabricated formulas which suppress thinking. We must turn to the creative, artistic process to generate fresh application of concepts. This involves *hypothesizing*—getting hunches and following them; *projecting*—entertaining a vision of the possibilities and options open to us; *anticipating*—relating to the universals and ultimates. The creativity which results is not mere embellishment or special effects or cleverness. It is the craftsmanship made possible by a

---

3. "Imagination in Preaching," in *Baker's Dictionary of Practical Theology,* ed. Ralph G. Turnbull (Grand Rapids: Baker, 1967), 23.

disciplined process of stimulating and shaping the imagination.

A few of the more well-known examples of preachers who show a lot of this and ought to be followed, in my judgment, are Buechner, of whom we have already spoken; Calvin Miller; Eugene Peterson; and Walter Wangerin. Wangerin is worth emulating because his preaching contrasts the explanatory mode which teaches and uses stories as illustrations and the evocative mode which tells the story and invites us to enter the imagistic world. The difficulty of evocative imagery becomes clear when we face the finding that at age five, 90 percent measure high in creativity but only 2 percent of adults measure high in creativity. What Percy Bysshe Shelley called "the world's slow stare" takes its toll on us devastatingly. We adults have become sophisticated and psychologically overcontrolled. We are further victimized by what has been aptly described as "the decay of the aura," first identified in *The Work of Art in the Age of Mechanical Reproduction* (1936). Mechanical reproduction is a boon that has greatly increased availability, but reproduction makes art too close, too available. Our jaded senses become overly passive and unaroused.

Thus G. Campbell Morgan labels imagination as the supreme work in preparation. John Ruskin taught that imagination works in three ways: it is penetrative, probing beneath the sensible surfaces; it is associative, for our purpose comparing spiritual with spiritual; it is contemplative. Andrew W. Blackwood also spoke of three kinds of imagination that are pertinent to preaching: descriptive—what's there; constructive—what's implied, and creative—what could be there. In all cases imagination should not be pure fancy. The radical pluralism of our time actually hinders creativity and imagination because it relates to no reality and so veers toward chaos and anarchy. We would argue that human creativity is a reflection of the *imago Dei*. God himself is intensely

and effectively creative. He ever confronts us: "Behold, I
show you a mystery!" We desire something more than a
kind of Sunday-supplement sermon. The God who creates and redeems has come into our lives.

> Heaven above is brighter blue,
>   Earth beneath is softer green;
> Something shines in every hue
>   That Christless eyes have never seen.
> —George Robinson

Dorothy L. Sayers has described creativity in terms of
the work of the holy Trinity: God the Father is the author
of the creative idea; God the Son is the expression of the
ideas through the consequent art forms of poem, painting, symphony, or sermon; God the Holy Spirit is responsible for communication to others. It is reassuring to
recognize that we are in league with the living God in
this creative process of communication that his sounds,
colors, and words mightily carry the message. It is fascinating to find depth in the ordinary. Christianity is
indeed a new way of seeing. Alexander Whyte, D. L.
Moody, T. De Witt Talmadge, Joseph Parker, and Clarence Macartney have used this special sight. Thomas
Guthrie was a pictorial preacher, as was Peter Marshall.

The preacher through this process brings home to the
hearts of the hearers the meaning and significance of
events and truths beyond our accustomed orbits. Pictorial language moves truth to touch the emotions as well
as to inform the intellect. Charles Jefferson held the congregation spellbound as he mused over possible reasons
why the nine lepers did not come back to thank Jesus.
George Whitefield so described a man about ready to
plunge over a cliff that Philip, Lord Chesterfield leaped
up and shouted, "Oh, he's gone! He's gone!" An old Welsh
preacher pursued the resolve of the prodigal with such
persuasive power that when he intoned "I will arise and

go to my father," two thousand people arose in their seats. We are certainly dealing here with some very special gifts in the body of Christ and yet there is encouragement for the most average of us as we trace the deterrents to and the development of creativity.

The Deterrents to Creativity

Creativity is not correlated with intelligence. Creativity can be cultivated and developed. If what we have described is needed and desirable for the Bible preacher, let's go for it. I love to read a good mystery story to challenge and stimulate my appreciation for the skills which make for suspense. Any Agatha Christie mystery will have to include a villain who, among all the possible suspects, has motive, means, and opportunity to commit the crime. Sherlock Holmes once solved a case by remembering that a dog had not barked. The British historian Herbert Butterfield remarked in illustrating the importance of imagination: "Detective stories may not be true to life, but it is the case in human affairs that the same set of clues, envisaged at a higher level of thought . . . may produce a new map of the whole affair, an utterly unexpected story to narrate."[4]

Friedrich Nietzsche spoke of "hidden paths to chaos." There are such for the preacher to avoid who would like to be more imaginative. We can all be sedated by the status quo, caught in the iron cage of modern life. Ralph Waldo Emerson said, "Whoso would be a man must be non-conformist." Our craving for conformity can tilt us invariably toward the path of least resistance. We don't dare let go of the trapeze because we are slavish imitators. This is why styles and fashion exert such decisive influence on us. We want to be in step. A much admired seminary professor had been wounded in the First World War and walked with a drooping right shoulder. A whole

4. Herbert Butterfield, *Christianity and History* (London: Fontana, 1949), 25–26.

generation of graduates from that school showed a marked tendency to walk with a drooping right shoulder. As surely as Watchman Nee clicked his dentures when he prayed, his admirers clicked when they prayed, dentures or no dentures.

There are many things, mostly our own bad habits, which stifle creativity. We need to oil the wheels of the cart. Good ideas can be lost if we don't jot them down when they come in the unexpected moments. They may be recorded and then lost in a sloppy filing system. Creativity may even be lost because we force it into an overemphasis on technique. Our technique can become an end in itself as it was in classic Greek drama or it tended to be in German music and Italian painting.

Above all, we need to be open to the new idea, the unexplored trail, the risk. It is exciting to see some of my students dedicate themselves to the pursuit of freshness and creativity in ministry and in preaching. The triumph is that insight, that single, seminal idea. The conception of that idea is a glorious moment—but to experience it we must shake loose from and shrug off the tyrannies and bondage of this present evil age.

The Development of Creativity

There are specific variables which make up creativity's equation. In all things imaginative, we are dealing with the capacity to see, and so we must first learn to see. William Blake even argued that "we are what we behold."

There is so much to be seen. Do we notice? Near the Madeleine in Paris on a lovely spring morning, two beggars were ensconced. One had a sign which read, "Blind from birth," but no one paid any attention to him. The other beggar had a sign with the words, "You can see the spring; I cannot." His cup was flooded with money. But how many in fact saw the spring?

Nathaniel Shaler has related his indebtedness to a

professor under whom he studied at Harvard. The professor gave to Shaler a small preserved fish with the assignment to study it. After an hour Shaler was ready to report, but it was demanded that he continue to study the fish for two weeks over several hundred hours. Shaler was amazed to find how much he could learn. With our fast-paced schedules and appointment books as thick as telephone directories, will we ever take time to see?

My father was raised in the north woods of Minnesota. I was always amazed by how much his trained eyes could see as we walked through a forest. We need to study great art and sculpture and all of nature. Jesus saw people with the insight of both complete knowledge and understanding love. He truly respected his hearers in the literal meaning of the word *respect* (i.e., to look again). We pass so many people without truly noticing them.

> To see a world in a grain of sand
> And heaven in a wild flower,
> Hold infinity in the palm of your hand,
> And eternity in an hour.
> —William Blake

Like Elisha's servant at Dothan (2 Kings 6), we need our eyes opened.

Truly seeing means keeping our memories green. The Nobel laureate French writer François Mauriac warned that marks left by one individual on another are eternal. In one sense we are to "forget those things which are behind" (Phil. 3:13), lest they preclude progress. On the other hand, our past contains treasures in witnessing God's work in us. "Forget not all his benefits," commands Psalm 103:2. Alyosha in *The Brothers Karamazov* says to the boys that "there is nothing higher and stronger and more wholesome and good for life in the future than some good memory, especially a memory of childhood, of home. People talk to you a great deal about your education, but some good sacred memory, preserved from childhood, is perhaps the best education."

Second, we must follow after reading. One of the most important ways to develop imagination is to read good books. Literature refines our sensibilities and nurtures creative power. Francis Bacon maintained that conversation makes the ready man and writing the exact man, but reading makes the full man. His experience was that some books you taste, others you swallow, and a very few you taste, swallow, and digest. Every preacher should have a systematic reading program with a balanced mix of many kinds of good material.

Frederick Norwood observed that sermons like rivers require a vast watershed. It is quite clear that fewer and fewer seminarians have a classical education with any broad conversancy with the great books. Joseph Sittler relates poignantly that Christians are not fulfilling their intellectual obligation to use the arts: "We are simply not cultivated people in our time. Of the old church an ancient historian said: 'The church in the first three centuries won the empire because they outlived it, outthought it and outdied it'—including intellectual and artistic achievement. But much of the intellectual and aesthetic life within the contemporary congregation is simply contemptible. Is the price of piety stupidity?"[5]

It should be remembered that the Bible has been a greater influence on literature than all other forces put together. Think of almost any truly immortal work of prose or poetry—Milton's *Paradise Lost;* Thomas Mann's trilogy on Joseph; Rudyard Kipling's *Road to Endor;* Dryden's *Ahithophel* or *Rizpah.* The preacher should be a lover and a reader of literature. T. S. Eliot, the most influential writer in the English language in our time, wrestles with the theme of conversion. John Ciardi lifts

5. Joseph Sittler, *Gravity and Grace: Reflections and Provocations,* ed. Marie Detloff (Minneapolis: Augsburg, 1986).

up the chief value in reading poetry as the way it gives vicarious experience and stretches our capacities for life. John Donne, William Wordsworth, William Cowper, Alfred, Lord Tennyson, Robert Browning, and Robert Frost fuel the furnace of imagery and style. Much modern fiction only clutters the mind with sensuality and licentiousness. But there is great profit in Charles Dickens and Anthony Trollope, to say nothing of twentieth-century novelists who have given us extended series of studies of the times and of human nature (e.g., John Galsworthy's *Forsyte Saga* or C. P. Snow's *Friends and Strangers*). An especial joy is Anthony Powell's multi-volume study of British life before and through World War II. Ethnic writers and dramatists and lesser known authors such as Barbara Pym are of immense value in their characterization of people and worth serious pondering of their styles of expression and communication. Good advice is: if you want to be an artist, study great paintings. If we want to be pictorial and effectively imagistic, let the masters teach us.

Third, we must allow ample time for creative brooding. The incubation of ideas cannot be rushed. Creativity takes blocks of choice time, not leftovers. Isaac Newton was asked how he solved a problem. His reply was: "I keep it before me." For some it must be solitude in the country or by a lake. Others do better in the city park with people and children about. Our styles and patterns are as diverse as our personalities, but there will be no creativity without ordering our lives beyond the routine and the television. Frost stepped out his door and "Stopping by Woods on a Snowy Evening" was born. René Descartes brooded before the fire. Newton allegedly contemplated the apple. Edward Gibbon sauntered through ancient Roman ruins. Thomas Hobbes always carried pen and ink. We owe it to our Lord and to his flocks to craft messages from the Word which evidence thoughtful attention to communication. Let the offense not be in the staleness of our work.

Fourth, our odyssey must involve a desire for careful, as well as creative, use of words. May God deliver us from degenerating into becoming mere purveyors of words, those who "darken counsel with words without knowledge" (Job 38:2).

I love John F. Kennedy's tribute to Winston Churchill, of whom he said: "He mobilized the English language and sent it into battle." We need to see words as ignition devices. The tendency is to live by catch words, but how we need to be burdened to cautiously use trigger words, which may have connotations that do not communicate what we mean to say. Fred Craddock recommends that we immerse ourselves in what Scripture says about words as in Isaiah 50:4–6 and 55:10–11; Matthew 12:33–37 and Romans 10:14–17.[6] Read from the masters of language and just listen, especially to children. Comb through your messages for words and expressions which are vague and hard to understand.

Listen to great music and notice the prominence of the theme. Compositions such as Franz Schubert's *Serenade,* Louis Gotschalk's *Lost Hope,* Richard Wagner's *Lohengrin,* Franz Liszt's *Hungarian Rhapsodies,* or Ludwig van Beethoven's *Moonlight Sonata* can greatly abet imagination. Read Shakespeare aloud to feel the power which has had such an amazing influence on the English language. Moreover, he makes twelve hundred references to Scripture in his thirty-seven plays. Do not ignore his magnificent sonnets, particularly those numbered 129 and 146.

The issue of creative preaching draws us to the inner resources of God. Dag Hammarskjöld, whose mystical kind of Christian faith makes *Markings* a worthwhile

6. Fred Craddock, *Preaching* (Nashville: Abingdon, 1985), 198–200.

reading challenge, says in his diaries, "In a dream, I walked with God through the deep places of creation." It was that sense of what God had done and was doing that inspired and ignited his spirit. To communicate this sense must be one of the contemporary preacher's deepest desires and greatest longings.

10

How Then Shall We Conclude?

The Issue of Intentionality

T he conclusion of the sermon is where our intention or central idea should come into the clearest focus. Yet the conclusion of the sermon is the weakest part of American preaching today. Not only among neophyte preachers in homiletical laboratories, whom I hear by the hundreds, but out in the churches, the fuzzy conclusion is the most serious symptom of the contemporary sickliness of preaching. Of all the flies in the homiletical ointment, this is the most vexatious.

Jesus tells us of the ridicule heaped on a man who began to build but was not able to finish (Luke 14:30). In many a sermon the preacher seems to lose the way. The message may begin promisingly and proceed powerfully, but there doesn't seem to be enough steam in the boiler to conclude effectively. Like a Fourth of July rocket it goes up, but then down it plummets ingloriously. It is an incoming plane which can't find the runway and continues to circle. How many times we have all felt that of our own preaching—how do we get down? For what is called "the fatal final third," some specific proposal and action need to be forthcoming. John Killinger quotes Herman

Melville regarding the enormous power in the tails of great whales: "Other poets have warbled the praises of the soft eye of the antelope, and the lovely plumage of the bird that never alights; less celestial, I celebrate a tail."[1] We're celebrating the tail in this chapter.

The sermon must move resolutely to the conclusion, lest it remain limpid as a lilied pool. G. Campbell Morgan wisely admonished, "Don't spend so much time getting your guns into position that you have to finish without firing a shot." Of Samuel Johnson it was observed, "He knew how to end as well as how to begin." This was indeed an enviable strength and one which every preacher should desire to emulate.

One of our great problems here has to do with having enough time. Pressed for time from every quarter, the preacher doesn't have much of it left for the conclusion and banks on having enough momentum through the Holy Spirit to improvise the wrap up. This seldom works, and we can't count on it. This is where preaching is so different from lecturing. The preacher must carefully craft that conclusion as absolutely critical for communication.

We must save ample time for the conclusion. While it should be relatively brief, it must be well shaped. Blessed is the preacher whose train of thought has a caboose. Rambling must be tightly reined in if we are to give a zinger to the last as we should intend to do. John Stuart Mill held that on all great subjects, something remains to be said. We can't say all that we want to say on a theme, but must pull it together and conclude strongly. The average Sunday morning sermon has forty-five hundred words. This means in an average lifetime the preacher speaks 8.28 million words in his sermons. That is doubled by Sunday night and tripled by a midweek service. In all of this the preacher can slosh out words.

1. John Killinger, *Fundamentals of Preaching* (Philadelphia: Fortress, 1985), 92.

We must learn how to hone the conclusion or we will seem a fanatic who loses sight of the goal but redoubles the effort to get there. Fuzziness in focus or the virtual absence of a finishing movement are catastrophic in preaching.

I recommend to my students that they spend two-thirds of their time on the last one-third of their message. At any sales convention or conference, the bulk of the time is spent working on the last five minutes of the salesmen's presentations, and for good reason. We generally are in grave danger of lumbering a half generation behind our culture, and one way to catch up is to recognize the necessity of a prompt and polished ending. Wasting time on special pleading or trying to unravel the coils of specious logic at the end destroys impact in the age of the short cut. When a student was asked if he wanted to buy a dictionary, he replied: "No, I'm waiting for the film version."

Objectives in the Conclusion

Every conclusion shares certain purposes, and achieving these objectives will make the work of preparing for the conclusion worthwhile. The first of these basic objectives is that we want to affect closure. It is in the conclusion that the unity of discourse flowers in a satisfying sense of wholeness. Some sermons proceed with careful development in the early phases. Perhaps fifteen minutes will be devoted to the first main, then seven to the second main, a breathless three minutes to the last main, and a hop, skip, and jump remain for the conclusion. It is unsettling for hearers and leaves the impression of inadequate preparation.

Pastoral sensitivity impresses on us the immense importance of reinforcing the sermon's practical relevance in the concluding movement. Here is where there needs to be the final clarification of thought with regard to the big idea. Here is where we engage in calling listeners to a right response. This should not be protracted or painfully convoluted, but neither should it be hurried, for we cannot go all this way and then pull our punches. Both the minister and the congregation are the most weary at this juncture, but these are our last moments with our dear friends. We must take pains with these last words. They must be right. Killinger quotes Henry Sloane Coffin that "many sermons leave an impression like the delta of the Mississippi . . . they sprawl away, instead of coming to a clear destination."[2] If the introduction is like the porch or portico to the building, the conclusion is like the spire that looms up as an appropriate last impression, psychologically, structurally, and aesthetically.

Second, in affecting closure we want to achieve climax. In terms of the emotional outline here is where we look for crescendo. Our pace and emotional punch are crucial for communicative effectiveness. What is called in secular public speaking "the oratorical drive" does have its counterpart in the sermon. This is one of the most difficult challenges of the novice preacher. He frequently supposes he can move in a horizontal close. Preaching is not only to inform, it is to inflame with a power akin to that described in Acts 11:15: "As I began to speak, the Holy Spirit came on them."

Evidences of emotional starvation are among us. Our preaching has tended to become so cerebral. Certainly there are extremes and excesses to be avoided assiduously. I would thoroughly agree with James Joyce that "sentimentality is an unearned emotion." I am not calling for something louder or more boisterous but for an element of appropriate intensity as we come down the stretch.

Third, in concluding we want to build connections.

2. Ibid.

Glen C. Knecht likens the conclusion to the final tap the mason gives to the brick that nestles it firmly and squarely into place.[3] That last tap is necessary for several transitions to be effective. If we move to a closing hymn of worship or commitment, there has to be a sense of good connection. If we move into the service of Holy Communion, the conclusion must be established solidly. If we are going to mount the appeal, there must be appropriate configuration and contour in the conclusion of the sermon. Some of our difficulty today in the invitation stems from mushy conclusions. If the invitation is a kind of conditioned, automatic procedure it doesn't much matter, I suspect, but biblical preaching must seek a verdict. The only kind of proclamation known in the apostolic church involved persuasion, exhortation, and appeal. The ethical aspects of persuasion will be in view in chapter 11, but, as John A. Broadus says, "Where there is no summons, there is no sermon." By slow degrees the heart is moved, but there comes the moment when we must draw the net. John R. W. Stott well argues that authentic preaching involves both exposition and appeal. There can be no real exposition without appeal for action, just as there can be no appeal without exposition.[4] The clear interfusing of these ingredients sharpens our awareness of the significance of the conclusion for the sermon.

Options for the Conclusion

Preaching is the finest of the arts, and certainly the crafting of the conclusion is no prosaic task. David G. Buttrick reminds us that "conclusions are governed by

3. Glen C. Knecht, "Sermon Structure and Flow," in *The Preacher and Preaching: Reviving the Art in the Twentieth Century*, ed. Samuel T. Logan, Jr. (Phillipsburg, N.J.: Presbyterian and Reformed, 1986), 295.
4. John R. W. Stott, *The Preacher's Portrait* (Grand Rapids: Eerdmans, 1961), 55–59.

intention."[5] That is to say, the nature and shape of our
basic direction and purpose in the sermon will determine
the nature and shape of the conclusion. The conclusion
should be suitable for the developing sermon. Just as in
basic structural patterns, there are various options for
the conclusion. We will now consider those options.

Direct Personal Appeal

Joshua's address to Israel (Josh. 24:2–16) has a vivid
conclusion: "Choose for yourselves this day whom you
will serve" (Josh. 24:15). Several sermons in Acts are
superb examples of the employment of personal appeal.
The preacher is co-worker with the Holy Spirit at this
juncture in a particularly moving way, as we see in Acts
2:36–40. It is only the Holy Spirit who can cut to the
heart, but as in every aspect of preaching, the Holy Spirit
uses lips of clay as his instrument. Paul's stately address
in Athens is another case that should be cited, as Paul
drives home his hearers' duty to repent: "In the past God
overlooked such ignorance, but now he commands all
people everywhere to repent. For he has set a day when
he will judge the world with justice by the man he has
appointed. He has given proof of this to all men by raising
him from the dead" (Acts 17:30–31).

Practical Application

Many a congregation feels a great letdown because
there is nary a clue as to where they are to go from here.
The sermon may have been good up to this point, but the
listeners are abandoned prematurely. The angel left
Peter only after escorting him through all of the gates
and past all of the guards and out into the cool night air.
After all of the intricacies of the Sermon on the Mount

5. David G. Buttrick, *Homiletic: Moves and Structures* (Philadelphia: Fortress, 1987), 97.

our Lord closed with a masterful illustration of application (Matt. 7:24–26). There is a kind of inevitability about the conclusion, given the proper development of our proposition. To change that direction in the conclusion would require changing the whole sermon. Here our nerve must not fail, nor the fear of man intimidate us. Here we sharply take issue with film director Alan Rudolph's famous line, "Truth is whatever gets the most applause." The shoe may hurt, but we must put it on.

Summary or Recapitulation

Summaries can be exceedingly tedious and predictable. To always conclude, "Now we have seen . . ." is to fall into an unfortunate trap. Only in a very argumentative sermon or in a very fine-lined progression should it be necessary to take invaluable concluding moments for retracing one's steps. Running recap as one makes the respective points should be sufficient in almost all cases, thus leaving the opening for an unimpeded final thrust. If we haven't made the development clear by now, we shall not succeed in rescuing the sermon from incoherence with last-minute first aid. Recap reinforces the impression of too syllogistic a pattern. Any retracing in almost all cases should be far more subtle and suggestive. This technique is too heavy and should be avoided.

Appeal to Imagination

Henry Ward Beecher was great at painting a word picture. Visualize, for example, the judgment seat of Christ and the believer appearing to give an account or imagine the great white throne and those who come to stand before God in the final great assize. I would, on occasion, step down from the pulpit (with a lavalier or lapel microphone) to feel much closer to the people and speak in conversational tones. Feel the pathos of the eternally lost soul. Sense the anguish of the benighted of

Ephesians 2:12 who are "without hope and without God in the world."[6]

The Use of a Short Poem or Hymn Stanza

A couplet or quatrain of poetry may so succinctly capture the central thrust. Poetry should be memorized. This both fosters its effective use and cuts down on the amount that is used. To break vital eye contact in the closing moments of the sermon by reading long chunks of poetry or prose is suicidal. Do not overlook the hymn stanza; what is more moving than "When I survey the wondrous cross on which the Prince of Glory died" for the crystallization of the response to the preaching of "Christ crucified"?

A Final Illustration

What has been called the "elusive" illustration is never more so than in the conclusion. It is possible to have too much of a blockbuster here, a picture so huge that the rest of the sermon is forgotten. This is not a common problem, but we must be cautious for a good tear-jerker can utterly wipe out the real thrust. The illustration should never be too long or it can get away from us. Pare down unnecessary details. An example of the sort of story which might be effective is the sculptor Bertoldo di Giovanni's warning to the young Michelangelo about the danger of dabbling. Coming into the studio one morning he saw his gifted protege chiseling on an insignificant piece of statuary. He picked up a sledgehammer and smashed it, saying, "Talent is cheap, dedication is costly." One does not need to multiply many words in the amplification of that point. Let it sink in.

6. James M. Wall, "Seeking and Embodying Our Hints of Truth," *Christian Century* 105 (June 8–15, 1988): 563. Wall likens this appeal to strikingly simple yet communicative cinematic images in some modern films.

An Apt Quotation

Quotations are often used to add punch to a conclusion, although Buttrick enters a serious caveat about the introduction of another voice at this important point, saying it makes of the preacher a ventriloquist's dummy. In general Buttrick feels the more conventional conclusions "intrude on direct discourse and therefore disrupt consciousness."[7] Again, one would wish Buttrick documented his idea about the field of consciousness as when he asserts that "if a speaker tells an audience about carrying his dog out for a walk, 95% of the audience will picture nothing" or "research indicates that illustrations from the preacher's personal life never bring to mind similar experiences from their own recall."[8] It is safe to affirm that overuse of any one technique would be unwise and that in general many preachers use too many quotations. But just the right one can make a point forcefully.

Coming Back to the Introduction

Even Buttrick will concede that "there is some indication that a closed-circle conclusion to a sermon will lift and frame in consciousness."[9] If we begin with an illustration or opening wedge, we can return to it in the conclusion and capitalize on binding elements. If in a sermon on the good Samaritan, I start with a point of contemporary contact—the so-called bystander effect[10]—I can return in my conclusion to that same bystander effect. Not all introductions and conclusions can be correlated in this way, but this is basic strategy which has considerable merit.

7. Buttrick, *Homiletic,* 105.
8. Ibid., 27, 142.
9. Ibid., 105.
10. R. Lance Shotland, "When Bystanders Just Stand By," *Psychology Today* 19 (June 1985): 50–55.

Personal Testimony

The inclusion of intensely personal reference always requires thought. In a sermon out of Daniel 3 on "When Nonconformity Is Necessary," I came down the stretch with the truth that, while God has not promised always to deliver us from the fiery furnaces of life, he has promised to meet us in the trial. Rather than using the experiences of others, either biblical or classical, I felt it important to share a fiery furnace which my wife and I have experienced, not in gory detail but quite existentially. My pastoral instinct is that there is a place for personal testimony, especially if it is not invariably implying or stating that we have been above or conquered over a particular trial.

Some Concluding Suspension

We need to finish and polish, but sometimes we need to open-end in a thoughtful way. Perhaps we shall end with a question, as did Arthur Gossip in his sermon, "In a Time of Change": "Always there will be two of us. And who can be lonely or dissatisfied, or afraid with Jesus?" Perhaps we may close with the simple reiteration of the text. The surprise ending like the surprise endings in the short stories of Guy de Maupassant ("The Necklace") or William Sidney Porter under the pen name O. Henry ("The Gift of the Magi") can occasionally be used in preaching.

Opportunities in the Conclusion

Our opportunity in the conclusion presents a staggering challenge. Here is where the richness and power of the Word of God can go into overdrive. At the city hall in Glasgow, Scotland, there were inscribed over the main entrance for generations the words: "Let Glasgow flourish by the preaching of the Word." After World War II the building was renovated, and the ancient city motto was shortened to: "Let Glasgow flourish." Modern streamlining had eliminated what was absolutely vital. We must not so streamline our conclusions as to omit or miss the clear, pungent thrust of the preached Word.

I do not think we can leave a congregation of hurting souls in the swamp. I contest the idea that lovers never speak negatively or doubtfully. The Word is a two-edged sword which both cuts and heals. But surely we can hardly, as ministers of the new covenant, preach law without gospel. We need both, but we cannot leave our people without a word of hope. This may be the last message someone hears. If the text ends in the slough we have every right to view it in its larger context and speak to the ravenous hunger of our people for some affirmation of hope and good news.

We must beware of pile-on in the conclusion which adds a little and then a little more and successfully blurs or obscures the point. We need to be on guard against the double conclusion which splits the focus. We need a straight-line conclusion—a simple and direct word. We may lose the people if our course is crooked as the Jordan. Don't add new material in the conclusion and, in effect, make it a pseudo-main. Quit while the congregation is still wanting more.

Don't lace your conclusion with "Now in conclusion" or "Bear with me a little longer." Human minds are like parachutes, and they'll bail out with little provocation. Also, don't sock the flock. Be vigorous and probing but not rough or combative in the conclusion.

Reuel L. Howe in *Partners in Preaching* shares his findings from a survey of laypersons who were polled as to their sense of the preaching they hear.[11] Six items were ticketed regarding preaching:

1. Sermons often contain too many ideas.

11. Reuel L. Howe, *Partners in Preaching* (New York: Seabury, 1967), 26–33.

2. Sermons have too much analysis and too little answer.
3. Sermons are too formal and impersonal.
4. Preachers assume the hearer has more theological and biblical knowledge and understanding than he or she does.
5. Sermons are too propositional and have too few illustrations, and often the illustrations are too literary and not helpful.
6. Too many sermons simply reach a dead end and give no guidance to commitment and action.

These are appropriately targeted areas for the preacher who is eager for communicating the everlasting gospel. We can counter all of them in our conclusions. Certainly our conclusion should be no dead-end alley but an inviting thoroughfare to life more abundant in Jesus Christ!

11

When Does Persuasion Become Manipulation?
The Issue of Ethicality

The art of persuasion has been practiced in the human family since the beginning of our common history. The ancient Greeks were more self-consciously reflective on the nature of persuasive discourse than perhaps any other people.[1] While Greek rhetoric and oratory have their roots in Homer, it was the rise of the city-states which gave new importance to skills in communication and persuasion. Suasion technique is always critical in a democratic or egalitarian society.

High regard was accorded the individual who could speak clearly and argue persuasively. Both Socrates and Plato, with their elitist and monarchial inclinations, generally disdained rhetoric and persuasion. Plato, indeed, dismissed them as "flattery." In *Phaedrus* he analyzes the three ways in which language affects us, but he is not alone in expressing considerable qualms about the misuse of persuasion.[2]

---

1. This reflective tendency is most engrossingly set forth in Isidore F. Stone, *The Trial of Socrates* (Boston: Little, Brown and Co., 1988).
2. Plato, *Phaedrus*, 260–63.

Aristotle in his *Rhetoric* takes the position that "rhetorical study, in its strict sense, is concerned with the modes of persuasion. Persuasion is clearly a sort of demonstration, since we are most fully persuaded when we consider a thing to have been demonstrated." In fact, Aristotle defines rhetoric as "the faculty of discovering in the particular case what are the available means of persuasion."[3] The persuader, according to Aristotle, utilizes three avenues of approach:

1. Argument for the intellect, the skilled marshaling of facts and logic. The communicator must beware of vague generalities, unsupported assertions, and faulty reasoning. General statements need to be advanced and extrapolated with accurate inferences. Richard Weaver in *The Ethics of Rhetoric* traces historical patterns of argument and observes that modern man's prodigious egotism and provincialism are expressed in argumentation that seeks immediate effect rather than ultimate truth.[4]
2. Appeal to the emotions, the inescapable necessity of confronting the reality of feeling, mood, and predisposition. Aristotle in book 2 of *Rhetoric* identifies a dozen emotions in a great exposition Lester De Koster calls "the Psalter's pagan counterpart. . . . [T]he preacher determined to mold feelings to divine purposes will find Aristotle an inexhaustible resource."[5]
3. Assurance of character. This is the most indispensable for Aristotle. We have already noted his comment that persuasion is achieved by the speaker's

3. Aristotle, *Rhetoric*, 1.2.

4. Richard M. Weaver, *The Ethics of Rhetoric* (Chicago: H. Regnery, 1953); Richard M. Weaver, *Ideas Have Consequences* (Chicago: University of Chicago Press, 1948).

5. Lester De Koster, "The Preacher as Rhetorician," in *The Preacher and Preaching: Reviving the Art in the Twentieth Century*, ed. Samuel T. Logan, (Phillipsburg, N.J.: Presbyterian and Reformed, 1986), 306–7.

personal character. We believe good men more fully and more readily than others.[6]

Greek concentration on rhetorical theory led to considerable ornamentation. The plain style yielded to the more robust middle style, and in many places, the turgid grand style was in vogue. The Asiatic school of orators was particularly extravagant. The history and practice of persuasion justifies both the establishment of rhetoric as one of the great ideas of the western world and the observation by Mortimer J. Adler and associates: "In the tradition of the great books, rhetoric is both praised as a useful discipline which liberally educated men should possess, and condemned as a dishonest craft to which decent men would not stoop."[7] Thus *rhetorical* in many quarters is an epithet with derogatory connotation, and there is an old saying that oratory is saying nothing but saying it better. Listeners are put off if it's too slick or too smooth. Weaver argues that the speciousness of the old rhetoric which is spread-eagle and high-flown arouses antipathy today, not indifference, though the success of some in the current political arena may cause us to qualify Weaver's judgment at this point. But where will communicators find their place if they wish to express truth with both ethical sincerity and rhetorical competence?

The Legitimacy of Persuasion

People today are wary of persuasion, and well they might be, for we are drowned in it. It is estimated that two thousand persuasion messages come to each of us daily. By the time of high-school graduation, the young person has watched more than 350,000 television com-

6. Aristotle *Rhetoric* 1.2.
7. *Rhetoric* in *Great Books of the Western World,* ed. Robert M. Hutchins and Mortimer Adler (Chicago: Encyclopaedia Britannica, W. Benton, 1952).

mercials. People today, notes Bill Hybels, are "bom-
barded by persuasive advertising campaigns, and after
awhile they learn how to put up defenses, to say to themselves, 'I'm not going to let this get to me.' "[8] The insecure
are most susceptible to the persuaders, and we all feel
exploited. The 910 persons who took their own lives at
Jonestown remind us of how human beings can be
manipulated by sharp operators without principle.

Our consuming desire is to present the truth of God
so as to see lives changed by Jesus Christ. Utterance is
part of the process in a fierce battle for the minds of men
and women. Beyond the intrinsic preparation for preaching to ascertain the content-truth of Scripture, we face
the weekly challenge of the extrinsic preparation to
determine the form, structure, and arrangement of the
communication. Both aspects of preparation are totally
dependent on the leading and guidance of the Holy
Spirit.

In the Gospels we are moved by the gentle persua-
siveness of Jesus. Apostolic preaching was always for a
verdict. A careful study of the verb *peithō* (to persuade)
shows how vital this was in the ministry of Paul:

Acts 13:43: Paul and Barnabas "urged them to continue in the grace of God."

Acts 18:4: Paul reasoned, "trying to persuade Jews and
Greeks."

Acts 19:8: Paul argued "persuasively about the king-
dom of God."

Acts 26:28: Agrippa asked Paul, "Do you think in such
a short time you can persuade me?"

Acts 28:23: Paul declared the gospel, "trying to convince them about Jesus."

8. "Turn the Gospel Loose: A Conversation with Oswald C. J. Hoffman and
Bill Hybels," *Leadership* 6 (Fall 1985): 20.

2 Corinthians 5:11: Paul said, "Since we know what it is to fear God, we persuade men."

In 1 Corinthians 2:1–5 it is obvious that Paul did not see the exposition of the truth of God as the sum total of his responsibility. There had to be persuasion also, as there must be any time we move on the citadel of the human will. Richard Roberts affirms that "it is our calling to persuade, and if it be, to convince. That is not preaching which is not preaching for a verdict." Nor does John A. Broadus overstate the case when he says that "the chief part of what we commonly call application is persuasion. It is not enough to convince men of truth, nor enough to make them see how it applies to themselves, and how it might be practicable for them to act it out—but we must 'persuade' men."[9] Raymond W. McLaughlin quotes George F. Sweazey that our advantage in evangelistic preaching is that we may spend time for persuasion.[10] Adds Richard R. Caemmerer, "Persuasive speech isn't just for entertainment. It makes a difference in people."[11]

The people we face have been essentially cut off from ideas and values we formerly could take for granted. The corrosion of traditional morality, the disparagement of virtue, and the erosion of language make our task difficult. What Robert Bellah describes as "the waning of cultural vitality" is all too apparent. The sense of obligation has been drastically reduced and the deferral of gratification is not appealing. A utilitarian morality of self-interest predominates. The task would be impossible were it not for one factor—the Holy Spirit.

---

9. John A. Broadus, *On the Preparation and Delivery of Sermons* (San Francisco: Harper and Row, 1979), 215.

10. George F. Sweazey, *Effective Evangelism* (New York: Harper, 1953), 159, quoted in Raymond W. McLaughlin, *The Ethics of Persuasive Preaching* (Grand Rapids: Baker, 1979), 55.

11. Richard R. Caemmerer, *Preaching for the Church* (St. Louis: Concordia, 1959), 53, quoted in McLaughlin, *Ethics of Persuasive Preaching*, 55.

The Limits of Persuasion

All who would be conscientious communicators of the gospel could profitably read McLaughlin's *The Ethics of Persuasive Preaching* and Emory A. Griffin's *The Mind Changers*.[12] There are limits to be observed and some crucial lines to be drawn if we are going to be persuasive but not manipulative. Griffin goes to the heart of the matter in his axiom: "Any persuasive effort which restricts another's freedom to choose for or against Jesus Christ is wrong."[13] This principle should operate in three areas bearing on persuasion.

First, fairness and honesty must control our use of the materials of discourse. We must not overstate what the text says. It is a great advantage to have the tools to handle the original language, for we need to be cautious with our data. In pursuing exposition of ideas, we employ supporting materials. These might include, as Otis M. Walter suggests, statistics, hypothetical examples, analogies, summaries, testimonies, and visual aids.[14] If all the parts and components of discourse are honest and fair, the discourse itself is more likely to be honest and fair. The question to continually ask is whether we are really true to the Word of God.

Second, we must watch our motives. Integrity is to be unimpaired, to be sound and whole. The totally pure motive is impossible to find, but we need to question our intent as we make embellishments and elaborations. We should desire to be able to say with Paul, "We are not trying to please men but God, who tests our hearts. You know we never used flattery, nor did we put on a mask

---

12. Ibid.; Emory A. Griffin, *The Mind Changers: The Art of Christian Persuasion* (Wheaton: Tyndale, 1976).

13. Ibid., 28.

14. Otis M. Walter, *Speaking to Inform and Persuade,* 2d ed. (New York: Macmillan, 1982), 17–33.

to cover up greed—God is our witness. We were not looking for praise from men, not from you or anyone else" (1 Thess. 2:4b–6). The obsession with results can dominate us and pre-empt concern for people. We move into the "I-it" mode rather than the "I-you" mode, making of people objects to be used. If only we can get someone to publicly respond to the invitation, then we are off the hook. Here is where we become unethical in our pursuit of divinely sanctioned objectives.

In the helpful article "The Credibility of the Preacher," Donald R. Sunukjian joins the issues well.[15] While competence is an important factor in perceived credibility, Sunukjian argues that even more important is the conviction that the speaker has admirable personal qualities and has the hearer's best interests at heart.[16] A blend of assertiveness, softness, and reasonableness seems felicitous. Warm facial gestures and pleasant tones help. The listeners know if we really care and speak because we love them. We love them too much to use them.

Third, we must guard our use of methods. The end never justifies manipulative means. Everett L. Shostrom contrasts qualities of the manipulator and the actualizor (true persuader). I summarize his thought to help us evaluate our methods in a specific situation (see fig. 11.1).

Coercion and too heavy-handed an approach constitute assault and interfere with the right to choose. God himself does not break down the door of the human heart. Jesus did not weep crocodile tears over Jerusalem. We deplore the demagogue who will not take no for an answer. If there is no free moral agency, there is no true ethical decision making, and if there is no ethical decision making, there is no morality. There are serious ethical implications in our use of persuasion.

15. Donald R. Sunukjian, "The Credibility of the Preacher," *Bibliotheca Sacra* 139 (July–September 1982): 255–66.
16. Ibid., 260–62.

FIGURE 11.1
The Manipulator and the Actualizor*

The Manipulator	The Actualizor
1. Deception, phoniness	1. Honesty, transparency
2. Lack of awareness, tunnel vision	2. Awareness, real interest, aliveness
3. Control, concealment	3. Openness, spontaneity, freedom
4. Cynicism, distrust	4. Trust, faith, belief

*Adapted from Everett L. Shostrom, *Man the Manipulator: The Inner Journey from Manipulation to Actualization* (Nashville: Abingdon, 1967), 50–51.

The Laws of Persuasion

The basis of persuasion must be in the possession and mastery of factual data. Reason and logic comprise the sine qua non of intelligent decision making. Decisions made under emotional duress may or may not be prudent. If the discussion involves more heat than light we have a situation of low visibility and are in grave danger. God himself invites us to come and "reason together" (Isa. 1:18). Stephen A. Douglas frequently took refuge in the excluded middle while Abraham Lincoln, with his extraordinary sense of perspective, almost invariably argued little from precedent but rather from first principles. There is no substitute for the right cause and the truth in any attempt at persuasion.

Yet persuasion clearly involves more than the stating of the facts. Emotion and motivation are the movers. Persuaders, says Harvard School of Education psychologist Howard Gardner, are people gifted with "interpersonal intelligence"—a set of abilities that enables them to understand and influence social situations. This is why thoughtful and appropriate use of humor can be so helpful in persuasion. Our purpose is not to create a joking environment, and some preachers certainly overdo it, but well-timed humor relaxes speaker and audience, softens controversy, disarms, and enhances receptivity. Rapport is essential for communicating the truth entrusted to us. Stuffiness is not a particularly effective persuasive technique. I recall witnessing to a woman whose chief complaint was that it seemed to her that Jesus had no sense of humor, that he was too dour. I put D. Elton Trueblood's *The Humor of Christ* into her hand.[17] When a sister scolded Charles Haddon Spurgeon for using humor in the pulpit, he is reported to have replied: "Well, Madam, you may very well be right, but if you knew how much I held back, you would give me more credit than you are giving me now." The prince of preachers was a person with interpersonal intelligence.

A professor at Arizona State University, Robert B. Cialdini, has given us a provocative study, *Influence*.[18] The author is an admitted professional in eliciting compliant behavior, and his arsenal of weapons of influence is enough to make one's blood run cold. He sees more unthinking compliance in the ever-accelerating pace and informational crush of our times. This book is like being given a tour of a Soviet missile factory. Here are the weapons used so adroitly by our adversaries and the shoals to be avoided if we are to take seriously the criteria for caring communication. So Cialdini's rules are particularly instructive to us as preachers:

> *The rule of reciprocation* creates a sense of obligation. The benefactor-before-beggar strategy is used by the Hare Krishna in giving a flower or a book before soliciting a contribution. We respond to repay a favor. This is behind some of the Christmas cards

17. D. Elton Trueblood, *The Humor of Christ* (New York: Harper and Row, 1964).

18. Robert B. Cialdini, *Influence: How and Why People Agree to Do Things* (New York: Morrow, 1984).

you receive from people you don't know and the free
sample technique. Even unwanted or undesirable
gifts are effective. But more crafty is the rejection-
then-retreat scenario, in which, when the raffle
ticket is refused, you sell the candy bar. We must
help people to see that this is a compliance technique
and not a favor. The rule of reciprocation is at work
in the so-called Stockholm Syndrome in which those
held captive by terrorists and criminals become sym-
pathetic to their captors.

The rule of consistency and commitment binds people
to past decisions which may not be relevant or wise.
We forget Ralph Waldo Emerson's wise dictum that
"a foolish consistency is the hobgoblin of little
minds." It manipulates so well because it provides
an easy-to-follow pattern that doesn't require thinking through new situations. The first to make public
commitment are the most obdurate against changing it. This is part of the dynamics of Alcoholics
Anonymous.

The law of social proof simply states that most would
rather imitate than initiate. No one cares for canned
laughter, but when many others laugh, we also
laugh. The more observers there are the less likely
we are to break ranks. So powerful is this reflex that
it is used to explain the tragedy of copycat suicides.
We must teach people how to say no!

The rule of liking is why companies are so successful
when they market their products at home parties.
The warm atmosphere of the home beats out the
impersonality of the store. Friendly, effusive, warm,
affirming compliance practitioners make us ducks
on a pond.

The rule of authority influences people because titles
and the trappings of power cater to our deferences
to supposed or actual authority figures. The jay-

walker in the pinstripe suit is like the Pied Piper of Hamelin. People will follow him but not the man wearing the sweater.

The rule of scarcity ascribes value to real or supposed rarity. We go to see a Mormon temple because it will soon be sealed. The limited-number technique gets many of us. Whenever our freedom to have something is limited, we have a greatly increased desire for it.[19]

In a world with a bewildering array of choices, in which most of our information is less than fifteen years old, we are vulnerable to exploiters. Our call as Christian communicators is not to blend into the woodwork in the present climate, but to become protectors of freedom and steadfast opponents of all exploitation.

The Language of Persuasion

John Dewey stated that no one ever thinks unless he or she is confronted with a felt difficulty. We face listeners who are people of faith, but we also face the hesitant, the hostile, and the indifferent. Strategies need to be formulated which will address the felt difficulties in each category. Preaching needs to diversify the appeals. Figure 11.2 reproduces Ronald E. Sleeth's suggestion for the best order of priority for using experience, authority, and reason to appeal to the several categories of hearers. The persuasive preacher needs to have in mind the various conditions in the congregation and regularly distribute the appeal.

David Kipnis and Stuart Schmidt conducted research to learn how dating partners and business managers sought to influence their partners or employees. There were three basic strategies—hard, soft, and rational. Hard means assertive, demanding. Soft means affirming,

19. Ibid., 29–260.

FIGURE 11.2
Categories of Hearers:
Varying the Appeal*

Believing	Doubting	Hostile	Indifferent
experience	reason	authority	becomes one of the others when interest is aroused
authority	authority	reason	
reason	experience	experience	

*Based on material from Ronald E. Sleeth, *Persuasive Preaching* (New York: Harper and Brothers, 1956).

caring. Rational means logical, bargaining. Which strategy was employed depended on the objective sought. Those who control resources, emotions, and finances have special advantage in a relationship. Such persons tend to use a hard strategy more often. This is called "the iron law of power." Anticipating resistance predictably increases hardness. Sometimes we expect resistance where none will significantly occur, especially if we do not have confidence or a fairly strong ego-construct. Social situations and biases can influence expectation also. The perception that "these people are different than I am" frequently leads to the idea that "they are not as reasonable as I am."[20] There is a need for hardness, softness, and rationality in the language of persuasion. You can identify all three in Paul's correspondence to the Corinthian church. The authors, while acknowledging the value in each of the three, find that the bottom line favors a reasonable, logical, and negotiating posture.

William James said that "what holds attention tends to determine action." A short story does not begin with a page describing the hills. We need to launch creatively and achieve a good blending and varying of elements. Sleeth counsels preachers not to sound like a train con-

20. David Kipnis and Stuart Schmidt, "The Language of Persuasion," *Psychology Today* 19 (April 1985): 40–46.

ductor calling off the stops. Nor does an audience want to be read to for thirty minutes.

"The very foundation of our concept of civilization is persuasion," according to Michael Novak. Vance O. Packard's *The Hidden Persuaders* shows us the great dangers in persuasion.[21] We have all been persuaded to do regrettable and irrational things. On the one hand Winston Churchill made England believe that Germany could be defeated and Susan B. Anthony persuaded Americans to adopt women's suffrage. On the other hand Adolf Hitler led Germany into the worst conflict in history and V. I. Lenin achieved Marxist revolution in Russia. Persuasion is both terrifying and an opportunity to move into the marketplace of ideas and, through the Holy Spirit, compete with false ideology and the tyranny of lies. Thank God we have the truth.

The faithful ministry of the Spirit who convicts the world of sin, righteousness, and judgment continues today and will until Jesus comes again. Look at Paul's discourse before Felix and Drusilla on "righteousness, self-control and judgment to come" (Acts 24:25). The Christian persuader works with God in the opening of human hearts to the gospel. As C. S. Lewis wrote of his conversion: "I felt myself being there and then given a free choice, I could open the door or keep it shut. I could unbuckle the armour or keep it on—I chose to unbuckle, to loosen the rein."[22] The result is a trophy of God's grace like the apostle Paul, who again and again could say: "I stand persuaded."

---

21. Vance O. Packard, *The Hidden Persuaders* (New York: D. McKay Co., 1957).

22. C. S. Lewis, *Surprised by Joy* (London: Fontana, 1955), 179.

12

How Can We Use Narrative More Effectively?
The Issue of Story

The Copernican revolution in homiletics it is called, the shift from the traditional, conceptual approach which no longer works because it fails to capture the interest of listeners.[1] Out of "vigorous new approaches to Biblical interpretation" requiring the dismemberment of the old homiletics, arises the new homiletics in which the object is no longer to find the message in the text; "rather, the text is now being viewed as a distinctive world, with its own unique shape and theological intention."[2] The focus is on preaching as storytelling, and it has become the rage in Protestant, Roman Catholic, and Jewish circles. Although by admission of its exponents this terrain is as yet relatively uncharted, here is the direction of the hour.

The whipping boy, of course, is the didactic sermon and rationalistic discourse. Now, we are told, style is more

1. Richard Eslinger, *A New Hearing: Living Options in Homiletic Method* (Nashville: Abingdon, 1987), 7.
2. Ibid., 8.

crucial to meaning than is content.[3] Eugene Lowry argues that we must move from the spatial paradigm, organizing ideas and propositional truths, to a time paradigm in which ideational content is supplanted by story. In other words, we need not a blueprint but a map. "Once a proposition is stated, it is done; closure has occurred, and only with great difficulty can one get things moving again."[4] The answer is to focus on events, not ideas or themes, and this means story.

Beyond doubt the new homiletic is saying something important which we ignore at great peril. Evangelical preaching must plead guilty, it seems to me, to being overly didactic with all too apparent a deemphasis on emotional and personal elements. The revolutionary character of the story model can teach us much. We who pride ourselves on preaching the whole Bible have, in the main, given scant attention to narrative in our preaching. If we have preached Bible biography and narrative we have tended to use a didactic methodology. In our visual society the story has infinite possibilities. Yet there is at this writing not yet a single substantive volume which approaches the preaching of narrative and the unique challenges of this genre from an evangelical perspective. Again we see the evangelical tendency to react rather than to act.

Before we hastily jump on this bandwagon, however, we must see that telling the story in homiletics rises out of a literary approach to Scripture and a narrative theology which evangelicals must judge to be deficient.[5] The new homiletic has risen from the new hermeneutic (which we shall consider in the next chapter) and has come to the fore for several reasons.

First, mainline theology maintains its vitriolic aver-

3. Ibid., 21.
4. Ibid., 65.
5. See the critique by Carl F. H. Henry in "Narrative Theology: An Evangelical Appraisal," *Trinity Journal* 8 n.s. (Spring 1987): 3–19.

sion to propositional revelation. The post-World War II
emphasis on "God's mighty acts" and rehearsal theology
(*Heilsgeschichte*) attempted to take refuge in the noncog-
nitive. Existential theology cannot accept the idea that
truth involves propositional correspondence with reality.
Therefore, a prominent Roman Catholic interpreter of
story theology tells us that "it is more important that the
story be interesting than that it be true."[6] He defines
narrative as the plotting of events with a set of purposes
dependent on context. His basic approach to Scripture is
that of a salvage operation to find what is compatible
with modern thinking. "Apocalyptic is incompatible with
our faith,"[7] so out it goes. Truth is changing, and, therefore, while he lists Dag Hammarskjöld, Martin Luther
King, Clarence Jordan, and Charles Ives as contemporary examples of effecting atonement, he cannot list
Mother Teresa because she does not show us any "new
way to make Christ present." This radical pluralism
revels in its uncertainty. There is no one simply true
story; "this lack of certainty is the good news"[8] since it
provides room for growth. The problem here is the total
surrender of biblical authority.

Second, mainline theology is in an "aesthetic stage,"
as my colleague Kevin J. Vanhoozer argues in a most
helpful article.[9] This means the author and content of
Scripture as such are subordinated to the present literary shape of the text; thus it loses objective meaning. Of
course when story is primary and the parables paradigmatic we have, in effect, a new canon. Much in Scripture
is not story. Should preaching be limited to story sections?

If we have imposed a spatial category, is there not a

6. Terrence W. Tilley, *Story Theology* (Wilmington, Del.: Michael Glazier,
1985), 186.
7. Ibid., 60.
8. Ibid., 165.
9. Kevin J. Vanhoozer, "A Lamp in the Labyrinth: The Hermeneutics of
'Aesthetic' Theology," *Trinity Journal* 8 n.s. (Spring 1987): 25–56.

danger in imposing a time category? Immanuel Kant would agree that these are both categories of the mind, as are others. Why is this an either/or? Jerome Bruner argues that there are two modes of thought, the paradigmatic (the more didactic or abstract) and the narrative (more aesthetic, dramatic, and symbolic).[10] Why should preaching not be both in the best sense? Are we seeing the pendulum effect dangerously operative?

Third, mainline theology reflects the enthronement of self as religious authority, thus resting authority in human experience. The unmanageable subjectivity of this position is seen in the range of resultant views— everything from a relatively conservative finding of Gabriel Fackre and his helpful *Christian Story* to the chaotic and totally horizontal work of Robert McAfee Brown, who seriously argues that the example of a nation which is ministering for Christ is Cuba.[11]

This state of anarchy and the crisis of language with reference to it have brought about some of the decline of preaching in our time. The preacher has lost confidence in the spoken word. No wonder conclusions are weak, indeed nonexistent, because the theology is weak. The continuing disparagement of rational consistency and empirical verification will only get us deeper into the mud. Aesop's *Fables* would provide as promising a matrix for the interplay of this subjectivity as the biblical stories. How are they really different? I hear Johann Goethe say: "Give me your convictions, not your speculations. I have doubts enough of my own." We can share the timeless truth of God's Word, and it is so timely. We shall hold to Scripture but we must not live in homiletical dinosaur land. The stupidity of the French generals early

10. Jerome Bruner, "Narrative and Paradigmatic Modes of Thought," in *Actual Minds, Possible Worlds* (Cambridge: Harvard University Press, 1986), 11–43.

11. Gabriel Fackre, *The Christian Story*, rev. ed. (Grand Rapids: Eerdmans, 1984); Robert McAfee Brown, *Unexpected News: Reading the Bible with Third World Eyes* (Philadelphia: Westminster, 1984), 139.

on in the Second World War is a warning of the great danger of not taking into account the changes in the real world around us and adapting our strategies accordingly.

The Appeal of Narrative

While I would not agree that stories are closer to reality than a discussion of ideas, as Peter Macky argues, I do concur in his endorsement of Robert Roth's observations that stories "come alive and jump to the complexities of life . . . for stories acknowledge the place of mystery as a natural element in reality."[12] We have an immeasurably rich resource in biblical narrative which we are hardly touching, and what we do in it is often quite unskilled and clumsy. After all, three-fourths of our Bible is the Old Testament and, according to one scholar, 75 percent of the Old Testament is narrative. This is to say nothing of the New Testament with its narratives and its exquisite parables from our Lord.

"Tell us a story, Daddy," my little children begged. No privilege is so great as teaching the soul of a child. The story is a hot medium. I was always interested to observe that in the "Children's Pulpit" segment of the morning service the adults were almost more interested than the children! What is a story? A story tells us of something that happened, beginning with a point of tension and finally leading to a resolution of that tension. Life is drama, and the story thus has a built-in mechanism for movement and progression. Lowry most ably depicts the homiletical "bind" and what it can do for us in preaching. The story begins with a discrepancy, a breaking of equilibrium and an analysis of this tension. The movement is from itch to scratch, from problem to solution. While

12. Peter Macky, "The Coming Revolution: The New Literary Approach to the New Testament," in *A Guide to Contemporary Hermeneutics: Major Trends in Biblical Interpretation,* ed. Donald McKim (Grand Rapids: Eerdmans, 1986), 278.

the disease-cure pattern is basic and not atypical of Scripture (paralleling law-grace in a real sense), there are many other patterns to be discerned. The "tell the story" movement is prone to considerable predictability. Story preaching is almost invariably a mode of indirect communication. Thus it has obvious appeal in a visual society, but it can easily become boring and tedious.

The narrative preacher is like the unknown monk in the European cathedral who drops the curtain from a sacred picture and confronts his charges face to face with the Crucified. Every preacher should pick up some audio tapes of Garrison Keillor's sketches of "Lake Wobegon," from his radio program, *Prairie Home Companion*. Here is a master storyteller and his widespread appeal bears analysis. Of the preacher's work, Keillor said in an interview some time back: "We don't need the minister unless he has something that the Spirit has put in his heart to say. We don't go to church to hear lectures on ethical behavior; we go to look at the mysteries, and all the substitutes for communion with God are not worth anyone's time. A minister who stands up and occupies twenty minutes of the worship hour only has to say one thing for the sermon to be worthwhile—just one clear image, one proposition that you can take home with you."[13]

"Why narrative now?" Fackre inquires. His answer is right on: "The climate is right. Storytelling thrives in times and places where imagination, intuition and affect assert themselves. The relative atrophy of these dimensions of selfhood in a culture dominated by modern science and technology . . . a quest for the recovery of the spontaneous . . . the challenge to left-brain dominance" all help us to see the appeal of story.[14] Story carries a sprinkling of emotional ginger which is most helpful today. Think of some of the more engaging television

13. Interview with Garrison Keillor, *Wittenberg Door* 82 (December 1984–January 1985), 15.
14. Fackre, *Christian Story*, 5–6.

commercials of recent years, like Clara Peller's "Where's the beef?" and Bartles and Jaymes's wine cooler spots with "Frank and Ed," whose creator advances a philosophy emphasizing the primacy of emotion both in advertising and in salesmanship. There is something for us to learn here.

While surely the gospel is not vaudeville, the Word of God is a red-hot iron. Some of our permafrost needs to give way to preachers with some fire in their bellies. Spectatorism must yield and story is an invitation to participation. The rediscovery of the story can bring us healthy variation and greater balance as well as grip our people anew with the power and appeal of the gospel.

Our Approach to Narrative

The preacher who would develop skills in handling biblical narrative must do more than "play Bibleland," as Krister Stendahl describes it. We need to get a real feel for this genre. One of the best helps is Robert Alter's classic, *The Art of Biblical Narrative*.[15] Alter is a Jewish scholar who has much to teach us of the new narratology. Alter is superb in showing the inadequacy of much of the conventional, critical scholarship with its tendency to splice and split the biblical text. He gives us a most practical definition of what constitutes a narrative event (an important issue for the preacher staking out his material): "A proper narrative event occurs when the narrative tempo slows down enough for us to discriminate a particular scene; to have the illusion of the scene's 'presence' as it unfolds; to be able to imagine the interaction of personages or sometimes personages and groups, together with the freight of motivations, ulterior aims, character traits, political, social or religious constraints, moral and theological meanings, borne by their speech,

15. Robert Alter, *The Art of Biblical Narrative* (New York: Basic Books, 1981).

gestures and acts."[16] Alter categorizes the techniques used in biblical narrative as characterization, reticence, the use of motif words and themes, the complementary functions of narration and dialogue, and the use of repetition.

The more traditional and standard approach in preaching narrative is certainly viable. The setting/story/significance or the story/principle/application outlines are risky. We tell the story and then share the equivalent of a television or radio commercial at the end. The better we tell the story the more likely our hearers are to become restive in the more labored effort for relevancy. Better suited to our purpose is the situation/complication/solution outline with indirect application as we go along.

Even a most tantalizing play or drama has acts and scenes punctuating the progression. The danger for the narrative preacher is losing the story line in his analysis. The use of a dramatic flashback in a longer narrative enables us to break into the action at a more dramatic point without starting at square one. This is most appealing in treating the books of Ruth, Esther, or Jonah in one message. We should beware of forcing any of these patterns on the text if it isn't really there. One can take a longer narrative (even a whole book in the Bible) and draw forth its principles, as here from the Book of Esther:

Principle 1: "God makes even the wrath of men to praise him" (the plot against Mordecai and the Jews)

Principle 2: "God works in all things for good" (Esther's courage, the king's troubled sleep)

Principle 3: "God will perfect that which concerns us" (the outcome for Esther, Mordecai, and the Jews)

Some homiletical techniques cannot handle narrative.

16. Ibid., 63.

Certain devotees of a particular method have told me they have never preached on the parables of Jesus because their method was not adapted for narrative. This is why we must be flexible and eclectic. When David G. Buttrick concedes that the Psalms and other hymnic material cannot be processed with his homiletic, it would seem to me that he's got to alter his approach in some way. Although some fascinating things are being done in narrative today, I would hate to hear only narrative, Sunday after Sunday.

Lowry makes some excellent suggestions for excavating the passage which serve whatever technique is employed:

1. Attend to every insignificant line.
2. Look between the lines to what isn't said.
3. Catch every encounter.
4. Bring data from your own parallel experience.
5. Move behind behavior to the motive.
6. Move behind the facts to prior dynamics.
7. Utilize the senses.
8. Switch identification.
9. Utilize active grammar.
10. Break into first and second person.[17]

Unless the preacher takes great care to establish his footing in the biblical narrative and retain his mooring through the process, the story can so easily become simply "my story."

The Aorta of Narrative Preaching

What is the meaning of the narrative? An effective storyteller will be heard for the sake of the vivid and engaging story he tells. Here is where our view of Scripture requires us to derive the basic meaning of the story

17. Eugene Lowry, *The Homiletical Plot: The Sermon as Narrative Art Form* (Richmond: John Knox, 1980), 89–95.

from Scripture itself. Sometimes the passage will overtly explain the meaning of the story. John 2:11 tells us the basic meaning of the first miracle which Jesus performed, and it fits with the overall purpose of the fourth Gospel (compare with John 20:30–31).

What is the intentional purpose of the author? Walter C. Kaiser, Jr., calls this the "central point of reference."[18] This is the thrust of the passage, and it is always easier to find in a didactic or poetic section. Frank Kermode offers us the consolation that "a text will offer, at some point a hint, an index or emblem of the whole—as a guide to our reading of the whole."[19] Some suggestions to help us find that meaning from within the text include:

1. Study the setting and larger context of the pericope. If it is part of the larger Abraham or David or Elijah cycles, for instance, we can obtain significant hints by seeing the action in its unfolding overall position.
2. Sometimes form itself can aid us in grasping the meaning. Patterns of repetition and arrangement can give us the clue we need.
3. Note the selection of details.
4. Ponder the climax of the story. This is usually a giveaway.

Certain central issues about the meaning of a passage, especially in the Old Testament, are hotly debated today and will receive attention in chapter 13—particularly the use of typology and how we preach Christ from the Old Testament. Certainly there is a sense in which the church is a story-shaped community. The telling and retelling of this old old story is an important part of community awareness. The emphasis on "telling" the story should ensure the essential orality of the communication.

18. Walter C. Kaiser, Jr., *Toward an Exegetical Theology* (Grand Rapids: Baker, 1981), 208.
19. Frank Kermode, *The Genesis of Secrecy: On the Interpretation of Narrative* (Cambridge: Harvard University Press, 1979).

The Adventure of Narrative

In making his case for the story and even our seeing the didactic sections as part of the story of redemption, Eugene Peterson quotes the literary critic Northrop Frye: "The emphasis on narrative, and the fact that the whole Bible is enclosed in a narrative framework, distinguishes the Bible from a good many other sacred books."[20] In the current climate much attention is being given to the parables of Jesus. "Without a parable he did not speak to them" (Mark 4:34, author's translation) reminds us of the degree to which our Lord himself used narrative. The parables of Jesus must not be given sole stress in our wrestling with these issues, but they furnish some key insights in the whole area of narrative.

Jesus, the skilled communicator, asked one hundred questions which are recorded, reminding us of Francis Bacon's observation that the skilled question is half of knowledge. Jesus used simile and metaphor (explicit and implicit comparison) as well as allegory (Matt. 22:1–14; John 15:1–10), but primarily he taught through the parable (putting one thing alongside another). Our Lord told fifty parables, about 35 percent of his teaching. The parable was intended both to conceal and to reveal (Mark 4:11), just as holding a smoked glass in front of the sun during an eclipse conceals in order to reveal.

The range of subject matter in the parables and short comparisons used by Jesus is quite striking. Herman H. Horne has done the classic study on which figure 12.1 is based.

The scope and sweep of the Savior's frame of reference is instructive. Through the early centuries the allegorization of the parables was extreme, with Augustine arguing that in the parable of the good Samaritan the innkeeper was the apostle Paul and the two pence were

20. Eugene Peterson, *Working the Angles: A Trigonometry for Pastoral Work* (Grand Rapids: Eerdmans, 1987), 83.

FIGURE 12.1
Subjects in Jesus' Parables and Short Comparisons*

inanimate objects	16	26%
plants	7	11.5%
animals	4	7%
people	34	55.5%

*From Herman H. Horne, *Jesus—the Master Teacher* (reprint ed.; Grand Rapids: Kregel, 1964), 86. Used by permission.

the two great commandments. Interestingly, John Chrysostom argued for a single meaning, and John Calvin fulminated against the medievalists for their spiritualizing. Adolf Jülicher built a case for the redress of abuse by maintaining that each parable had a single point and that a moral one. C. H. Dodd and Joachim Jeremias have urged us to put the parable into its setting and to see every part of the parable in relation to Jesus' purpose for telling it. The basic approach to the understanding and preaching of the parable has been set forth by Milton S. Terry:

1. Determine the occasion and the aim of the parable.
2. Analyze the subject matter and the imagery.
3. Develop the several parts and make prominent the central truth.[21]

Again we must be watchful of the setting/story/significance form. One esteemed preacher set the miracle story out of John 2:1–11 under three heads: believing prayer, obedient faith, and creative power. My question must be: Do we really have three sermonettes here? They are all true, but is there any grappling with the author's pur-

21. Milton S. Terry, *Biblical Hermeneutics* (New York: Eaton and Mains, 1883), 276–301.

pose, given in verse 11, for including this event in a carefully culled selection of but a few events?

The notoriously difficult parable of the workers in the vineyard (Matt. 19:27–20:16) affords us an opportunity to press toward an understanding of the purpose of our Lord in telling the story. It strikes me that Jesus in this parable is speaking to the spirit of 19:27 where Peter, the "American apostle," is really looking out for number one! Applying the hermeneutical hints already given, I would incline to a ladder-type outline in seeking to do justice to the details and setting of the story and to make the story live and intersect with our lives today. But I want to be sure that I move on to the climax and the full picture along with Jesus' own concluding interpretive sentence. I might incline to an outline something like:

  I. God has work for us to do—the landowner hires workers for the vineyard
 II. God has work for all of us to do—not all have the same opportunity, the same strength, or the same gifts, but there is work for us all to do
III. God has work for all of us to do in a covenant of grace
    A. Not a business transaction
    B. No basis for boasting to the latecomers
    C. Comparisons are odious

Doth God exact day labor, light denied?
....
They also serve who only stand and wait.
—Milton, *On His Blindness*

The ferment over narrative is fraught with immense peril if we drift rudderless upon the shoals of subjectivity, but it is filled with a great prospect for the people of God as we are awakened to the possibilities and potential of our rich narrative treasures.

13

When Shall We Preach Christ?
The Issue of Christocentricity

We may vigorously defend the authority of Holy Scripture—and we ought to do so—but then lose everything in the area of hermeneutics, the art and science of interpretation. (Hermes was the messenger of the Greek gods, hence hermeneutics.) The Bible is true but that fact is of no consequence if we do not press on to ask: "Now, what does it say?"

Historically hermeneutics has dealt with the principles and rules by which the various literary genres of Scripture are to be understood. These are the tools by which the preacher excavates the text. Generally we seek to understand the Bible as we would seek to understand any book. Taking into account the author's frame of reference and intention we give a literal, plain, and normal reading to the text, allowing for obvious figures of speech. Biblical preaching as we have defined it leans heavily on the Spirit-illumined skills of the conscientious interpreter.

One of the great beauties and glories of Scripture is to be seen in its perspicuity. It is meant to be understood; it is not obscure and ambiguous. Surely there are "some things hard to understand" (2 Pet. 3:16). J. I. Packer helps us in this matter with a choice quotation from a seventeenth-century Puritan named William Bridge: "For a godly man it should be as it was with Moses. When a godly man sees the Bible and secular data apparently at odds, well, he does as Moses did when he saw an Egyptian fighting an Israelite: he kills the Egyptian. He discounts the secular testimony, knowing God's Word to be true. But when he sees an apparent inconsistency between two passages of Scripture, he does as Moses did when he found two Israelites quarreling: he tries to reconcile them. He says, 'Aha, these are brethren. I must make peace between them.' And that's what the godly man does."[1] As Augustine said, "The Bible is like a river in which a child can swim and an elephant can wade." Any earnest, Spirit-led believer can understand and handle the Word. Study and meditation are required and should continuously be enhanced with more and more tools to give an ever-deepening and more satisfying understanding.

In recent years hermeneutics has come to involve philosophical and theological issues about Scripture itself. The new hermeneutic coming out of Rudolf Bultmann and Martin Heidegger holds that language itself is an interpretation and cannot be understood in reference to ancient texts as somehow embodying objective truth. Understanding is existential, involving a "hermeneutical circle" in which selfhood and the text come together in contemporary daily life (David G. Buttrick's "field of consciousness"). Anthony Thiselton, in a probing discussion of these issues, insists that if the ancient text is to come alive today and really strike home, two sets of horizons must come together, those of the text and those of the

---

1. J. I. Packer, *Your Father Loves You: Daily Insights for Knowing God,* ed. Jean Watson (Wheaton: Harold Shaw, 1986), June 21.

modern interpreter, and these must meet at more than a conceptual level.[2]

It is well that we are reminded that there is no such thing as "presuppositionless exegesis." J. D. Smart argues that the claim of absolute scientific objectivity in interpreting Scripture "involves the interpreter in an illusion about himself that inhibits objectivity."[3] Hermeneutics is not an exact science. We all bring our systems, traditions, prejudices, and sin to the task of understanding Scripture. This is one of the reasons why our understandings differ and in many cases are just wrong. But, conscious of our predilections and humbly eager to be taught of the Spirit, we can come to the text of Scripture for understanding.

Such a posture before the text is far different than the surrender of a transcendent God who speaks to us in objective truth. The new hermeneutic has essentially lost biblical meaning because it has too great an emphasis on self-understanding. The fruit has been hermeneutical confusion, a pitiful pluralism without focus. The preacher must retain confidence in the Bible we hold in our hands as objective knowledge. The Bible has status as revealed truth regardless of who approaches it or how. It has a life independent of my self-understanding. Its truth is not in flux.

Our task for preaching is to ascertain the meaning of the biblical text. Eric D. Hirsch, Jr., has made the crucial distinction between meaning and significance: "Meaning is that which is represented by a text; it is what the author meant by his use of a particular sign sequence; it is what the signs represent. Significance, on the other hand, names a relationship between that meaning and a

2. Anthony Thiselton, "The New Hermeneutic," in *A Guide to Contemporary Hermeneutics: Major Trends in Biblical Interpretation,* ed. Donald McKim (Grand Rapids: Eerdmans, 1986), 107.
3. J. D. Smart, *The Interpretation of Scripture* (London: SCM, 1961), 29.

person, or a conception or a situation."[4] The quest for
meaning is altogether foundational for the preacher who
would share the significance of the biblical text in today's
world.

Tension Points in Evangelical Hermeneutics

Behind the meaning of the text is the author's intent.
We need to bring every available tool to the task of
understanding the text in its context—grammar and syntax, archaeological and historical data (with good commentaries as helps and checks for us in the process), to
name but a few. Some passages will yield a clearer sense
of the author's intent than will others. We are dealing
with probabilities in any case. More difficult narrative
sections may be less probable than certain didactic sections where basic intent seems stated quite clearly. This
is where we see that hermeneutics is not an exact science, since godly interpreters will not always see the
matter identically. There is no infallible book which gives
the author's purpose in every passage. An important
safeguard for us in interpretation is the *analogia Scriptura* or what Scripture teaches as a whole and *analogia
fidei* or what the church has believed as a whole on this
matter. We must be careful not to impose categories and
concepts from later revelation upon the ancient text,
because we do believe in incremental revelation. Yet no
part or segment of divine revelation can ever contradict
another part or segment. The later builds on the earlier
in beautiful harmony as the venerable sacrificial system
of the Old Testament was replaced by the once-for-all
sacrifice of Jesus Christ.

The author's meaning in the text must not be assumed

---

4. Eric D. Hirsch, Jr., *Validity in Interpretation* (New Haven: Yale University Press, 1967), 8.

to be always simplex because intentionality is not always simplex. Any writer or doer (biblical or otherwise) may have fairly complex intentionality. Jesus performed miracles as an expression of his compassion, but more importantly to accredit his ministry and further to teach lessons and truths (Luke 5:24). The resurrection narratives have several purposes. In some passages it may be more difficult for us to understand the author's single intent, while in others we grapple with the possibility of multiple intentions. In any case, hermeneutical findings must all be justified from the text itself seen in its context.

Another critical issue in evangelical hermeneutics is how to distinguish in Scripture between the universals which are normative for all time and elements that are cultural and time-bound. We are dealing here with the "significance" part of the Hirsch definition. There may well be implications for us even in a very specific message for an ancient king, the nitty-gritty of which has no relevance. At the 1982 Summit 2 of the International Council on Biblical Inerrancy, J. Robertson McQuilken advanced the position that "every teaching in Scripture is universal unless Scripture itself treats it as limited." McQuilken raises seven helpful questions for the interpreter:

1. Does the context limit the recipient or application?
2. Does subsequent revelation limit the recipient or application?
3. Is this specific teaching in conflict with other biblical teaching?
4. Is the reason for a norm given in Scripture and is that reason treated as normative?
5. Is the specific teaching normative as well as the principle behind it?
6. Does the Bible treat the historical context as normative?

7. Does the Bible treat the cultural context as limited?[5]

These are obviously critical questions for the contextualizer in our own culture and particularly in the missionary context abroad.

Few areas have been more difficult for us than issues relating to the New Testament use of the Old. It seems to me overmuch to argue that the Old Testament writers fully understood all that they prophesied. The idea of multiple fulfillments of an Old Testament prophecy would seem to admit the possibility of an Old Testament writer not fully grasping the import of what he wrote. Is any writer or speaker fully conscious of total import? We do not lose control of interpretation by admitting that the prophets did not fully understand the times when their prophecies should be fulfilled (1 Pet. 1:10–12). Daniel wrote about the times (as in Dan. 9:24–27) and so clearly wrote about things he did not understand. Did any Old Testament reader of Psalm 16 understand this to be a prophecy of one who would die and rise again? How much did David himself understand? Did Balaam have a clear understanding of the two comings of Christ as prophesied (Num. 24:17–18)? Did Abraham really grasp anything of the real extent of his progeny as promised?

There is a kind of *sensus plenior* or fuller meaning of Scripture to be seen when the hitherto incremental revelation is made complete. Thus Packer argues that if God's meaning and message "exceeds what the human writer had in mind, that further meaning is only an extension and development of his, a drawing of implications and establishing of relationships between his words and other, perhaps later biblical declarations in a way

5. J. Robertson McQuilken, "Problems of Normativeness in Scripture: Cultural versus Permanent," in *Hermeneutics, Inerrancy and the Bible: Papers from ICBI Summit II,* ed. Earl D. Radmacher and Robert D. Preus (Grand Rapids: Zondervan, Academie Books, 1984), 230.

that the writer himself, in the nature of the case could not do."[6] This recognition is not to introduce any arbitrary element into our pilgrimage in quest of the meaning and significance of the text of Scripture.

In the final analysis we stand with the Reformers in believing that the whole of Scripture must interpret the parts of Scripture. While we wrestle with Daniel the sixth century B.C. prophet and weigh his prophecies with care in the light of his historical situation and his knowledge, we ultimately synthesize Daniel and Revelation when as futurists we speak of the endtime events. We believe in the unity of divine revelation because, though there were forty different human authors, there is one divine author. We bring Daniel, Joel, Zechariah, the Olivet Discourse, 2 Thessalonians, and Revelation together. Thus the New Testament, in the general understanding of the church through the centuries, must finally be decisive in our understanding of the Old Testament.

The Centrality of Christ

A critical test-case focus for several of these hermeneutical issues is the very practical question of when Christ is to be preached in the Old Testament.

"I hear very few sermons about Jesus" begins one recent and interesting lament from the liberal camp.[7] The Christian proclaimer, whether preaching from the Old Testament or the New, must present Christ as the ultimate frame of reference. The Christian proclaimer can preach no text in the Old Testament as a rabbi would preach it because the fulfillment of the promises has come in Christ and we live under the new covenant. The Christian proclaimer has a lifelong love affair with the

6. J. I. Packer, "Hermeneutics and Biblical Authority," *Themelios* 1 (Autumn 1975): 6.

7. Marcus Borg, "The Historical Jesus and Christian Preaching," *Christian Century* 102 (August 28–September 4, 1985): 764.

Old Testament, the Bible which Christ and the apostles cherished. But our preaching of any part of Scripture must stand within a clear sense of theological construct, and for the Christian proclaimer that construct is Christocentric.

In this sense all biblical preaching is doctrinal preaching. Our preaching is within a system of understanding. That theological construct should be the product of exegesis, biblical theology, historical theology, and systematic theology. The weakness of preaching without this sense of construct is painful to a congregation over time although they may not be able to pinpoint the exact locus of the problem. The lack of continuity and cohesion and the general inconsistency found in much preaching all bear witness that, while there may have been analysis, there has been no significant synthesis.

The Chicago Statement on Biblical Hermeneutics (1982) unequivocally states: "The person and work of Jesus Christ are the central focus of the entire Bible. We deny that any method of interpretation which rejects or obscures the Christ-centeredness of the Bible is correct."[8] This is how our Lord saw the Old Testament scriptures: "And beginning with Moses and all the Prophets, he explained to them what was said in all the Scriptures concerning himself" (Luke 24:27). Jesus said of the Old Testament, "These are the Scriptures that testify about me" (John 5:39). Apostolic preachers saw the Old Testament as fulfilled in Christ, and they preached Christ as set forth in the Old Testament (Acts 2:31; 3:24–25; 8:35; and other passages). Paul saw the Old Testament christologically (2 Cor. 1:20). Hebrews is a particularly vivid example of seeing the Old Testament from within the fullness of the New Testament revelation in Christ (for example, Heb. 10:7).

We do not possess a manual of Old Testament inter-

8. In *Hermeneutics, Inerrancy and the Bible: Papers from ICBI Summit II*, ed. Earl D. Radmacher and Robert D. Preus (Grand Rapids: Zondervan, Academie Books, 1984), 890–91.

pretation written by the apostles, as Richard N. Longenecker has well shown in *Biblical Exegesis in the Apostolic Period.*[9] Again we are impressed with the fact that hermeneutics is not an exact science. What is clear is that Jesus Christ as the eternally begotten Son of the Father is at the heart of "the eternal purpose of God." It is the Father's will that "in everything he might have the supremacy" (Col. 1:18). It is the continuing and faithful ministry of the Holy Spirit to glorify and bear witness to Christ. He is the only way to the Father, the one and only Mediator through whom we may be saved, as is asserted in John 14:6, 1 Timothy 2:5, and Acts 4:12. So Paul insisted often that he preached Christ Jesus the crucified Lord. The quintessential theme of the Christian proclaimer must be the Lord Jesus Christ. Charles Haddon Spurgeon said, that the true grandeur of preaching was to exalt Christ grandly in it. The history of preaching bears out Ronald Ward's contention: "If the preacher withholds the impartation of Christ, he is not preaching." What was true for the early fathers, the Reformers, the Puritans, John Wesley, and Alexander Maclaren is no less true for us. A sermon without Jesus is a garden without flowers.

The Centrality of Christ in the Old Testament

There is now much fruitful discussion on the relationship between the Old Testament and the New Testament (see the recent books by Walter C. Kaiser, Jr., and Thomas E. McComiskey, as well as the classic by S. Lewis Johnson.[10]) No one is any clearer than John Bright

9. Richard N. Longenecker, *Biblical Exegesis in the Apostolic Period* (Grand Rapids: Eerdmans, 1974).

10. Walter C. Kaiser, Jr., *The Uses of the Old Testament in the New* (Chicago: Moody, 1985); Thomas E. McComiskey, *The Covenants of Promise: A Theology of the Old Testament* (Grand Rapids: Baker, 1985); S. Lewis Johnson, *The Old Testament in the New: An Argument for Biblical Inspiration* (Grand Rapids: Zondervan, 1980).

when he asserts: "Christ is indeed to us the crown of revelation through whom the true significance of the Old Testament becomes finally apparent."[11] This is the crucial framework within which the preacher of Christ comes to the Old Testament. We shall analyze the incomparably rich deposits of truth which constitute our Old Testament under three categories.

Prophecies of Christ in the Old Testament. The most obvious christological ore to be mined in the Old Testament is direct messianic prophecy. The Bible has a unique body of predictive prophecy and promise. This has immense apologetic value but is also rich and full of practical truth for us. The Talmud maintains that "all the prophets prophesied only of the Messiah" (Sanhedrin 99a). It has been alleged that 456 references to the Messiah were identified in the Old Testament in the synagogue. Arthur T. Pierson spoke of what he called the Mosaic or germinal stage, the Davidic or growing bud stage, and the prophetic or full-grown flower stage. Canon Henry P. Liddon spoke of Isaiah as "the richest mine of Messianic prophecy." Ernst W. Hengstenberg's massive *Christology of the Old Testament* is still a useful tool in searching out the treasures of what the Old Testament predicates concerning the person and work of "the desire of all nations."

Pictures of Christ in the Old Testament. Less precise and determinate than actual prophecies of Christ, are types or pictures of Christ in the Old Testament. Johnson helpfully states that "typology is the study of the spiritual correspondences between persons, events and things within the historical framework of God's special revelation."[12] This presupposes a linear understanding of history. Johnson quotes B. F. Westcott that "a type presupposes a purpose in history from age to age."[13] Cer-

---

11. John Bright, *The Authority of the Old Testament* (Nashville: Abingdon, 1967), 112.

12. Johnson, *Old Testament in the New,* 55.

13. Ibid.

tainly some have been addicted to excesses in typology to the point that every pin in the tabernacle in Israel and every hair in the beard of the he-goat in Daniel are fraught with profound significance. But the reaction to these excesses has been too strong and there appears to be a return to a more balanced view that there are persons, events, institutions, offices, and actions which are pictorial. The Scripture speaks of types and tells us that "the rock was Christ" (1 Cor. 10:4). The Book of Hebrews uses typology as its basic hermeneutic. Certainly where the New Testament explicitly establishes the correspondence—as with Adam, the flood, or Melchizedek—we are on the safest ground. There can be no question about the brazen serpent, manna, the Passover, Jonah in the fish, or Hosea's marriage. Regarding cities of refuge, the life of Joseph, and the Jewish Sabbath and religious calendar, good sense and careful judgment assist us in perceiving aspects and nuances of our Savior's redemptive work.

Preparations for Christ in the Old Testament. God's saving work is everywhere in the Old Testament. In this holistic sense, all of the Old Testament prepares for and is fulfilled in Christ. We can't preach the Old Testament as if the fulfillment had not come. Much contemporary preaching from both Testaments tends to be strongly hortatory with a thin devotional overlay. The Bible is seen as the source of moral instruction primarily, with secrets for success, models of leadership, and similar helps. This is to miss the theological mainspring of Scripture, the divine intervention in Jesus Christ. It is within this framework that ethical and social responsibility become meaningful and realizable. The Ten Commandments are set forth in such a context: "I am the LORD your God, who brought you out of Egypt, out of the land of slavery" (Exod. 20:2–17). Apart from the redemptive acts of God, ours can only be the torment of an unattained ideal. The law is a schoolmaster to bring us to Christ (Gal. 3:24). There is no section or part of the Old

Testament which is not messianic in this critical sense. The expositor cannot leave the hearer with a moralistic aphorism or imperative, however needed. It is our privilege and joy to place the frame of Christ around the passage. God's purpose in Christ is creative, redemptive, providential, and eschatological, that is, he makes, saves, cares, and completes, and this is all in Jesus Christ. Christ is the critical issue.

It is in this sense that I understand Spurgeon's representation to a young preacher:

> Don't you know, young man, that from every town and every village and every hamlet in England, wherever it may be, there is a road to London? So from every text of Scripture there is a road to Christ. And my dear brother, your business is, when you get to a text, to say, now, what is the road to Christ? I have never found a text that had not got a road to Christ in it, and if ever I do find one, I will go over hedge and ditch but I would get at my Master, for the sermon cannot do any good unless there is a savor of Christ in it.[14]

The fact is that if it is baloney, no matter where you cut it, it is still baloney. Robert Capon has accused twentieth-century theologians of sometimes casting "flawless, perfectly matched, king-sized wedges of baloney" about. Buttrick's exercise in homiletical theology, *Preaching Jesus Christ,* is helpful to test the validity of some of our critique. As one whose "new homiletic" is squarely placed in the "new hermeneutic," it is not surprising that throughout this work he is historically skeptical and agnostic. He feels the sure facts of Jesus' life, miracles, and teaching cannot be certified.[15] Christology seems to flatten out. There is an oppressive horizontalism in the preaching.

Apocalyptic is dismissed out of hand as without mean-

14. Charles Haddon Spurgeon, "Christ Precious to Believers," in *Sermons* (New York: Funk and Wagnalls, n.d.), 6:356.

15. David G. Buttrick, *Preaching Jesus Christ* (Philadelphia: Fortress, 1988), 12.

ing to modern man (a curious misreading of our very apocalyptic times, in my judgment). "Christ is always a mysterious, symbolic figure."[16] In shedding his Barthianism Buttrick seems to have lost pretty much any transcendent element in the Lord Jesus. Jesus as personal Savior gets the back of the hand. Our proclamation must be social salvation. The apocalyptic imagery of resurrection past and future must be cut aside to uncover the kernel that remains, the notion of a new age which is dawning.[17]

Some of the old church fathers strayed into allegory of an outrageous kind. One saw the three white baskets of which the baker dreamt and told Joseph as the Holy Trinity and the bride's hair in the Song of Solomon as "the mass of the nations converted to Christianity." Another saw the four barrels of water in the Elijah cycle as the four Gospels. A later luminary saw the one ship on Galilee as the Church of England and "the other little boats" as the Nonconformists. Job's friends were heretics, his seven sons the twelve apostles (?), his seven thousand sheep God's faithful people, and his three thousand humpback camels the depraved Gentiles. A travesty! Yet Bernard Ramm observes that it was the Christocentricity in allegorical exegesis that kept it from being pure trash.[18] It must sadly be said that in the bypaths of the new hermeneutic Christology has been ravished and reduced. The critical issue in the church has always been, what do we think of Christ. He is the critical issue in all of history. Let our preaching faithfully and fervently reflect and radiate the biblical doctrine of Jesus Christ. He still saves![19]

16. Ibid., 21.
17. Ibid., 34.
18. Bernard Ramm, "Biblical Interpretation," in *Baker's Dictionary of Practical Theology,* ed. Ralph G. Turnbull (Grand Rapids: Baker, 1967), 103.
19. A striking new treatment of preaching the literary genre of the passage is found in Sidney Greidanus, *The Modern Preacher and the Ancient Text* (Grand Rapids: Eerdmans, 1988). Here also is a strong statement on the necessity of Christocentric interpretation: 118–19, 220–21, 305–6, 331–33.

14

How Can We Develop and Hone Personal Style?
The Issue of Originality

Our style in preaching is the way we do it, what works best for us. The stylus was originally a pointed iron instrument used for writing and it came to refer to our own way of writing. George Louis Leclerc de Buffon, the French stylist, said, "The style is the man himself." William Strunk, himself a master stylist, speaks of style as "that which distinguishes or is distinguished, the self escaping into the open." The Scriptures remind us that "we have this treasure in earthen vessels" (2 Cor. 4:7 KJV), and we are never in doubt that the marks of our own manufacture are in clear evidence in every message we preach.

Many influences have made us the persons we have become. In Abraham Lincoln we can see the cadences of the Bible, the subtleties of William Shakespeare, and the humanity of Bobby Burns. Winston Churchill steeped himself in the historians Edward Gibbon and Thomas Babington Macaulay, and we can see these men at work in the powerful language emanating from this master communicator. Paul Gericke has analyzed the preaching of Robert G. Lee, whose style was greatly influenced by Edwin M. Poteat and T. DeWitt Talmadge. His preaching style was characterized by clarity, energy, great elegance of expression, vivid imagination, and humor.

Style has been called "the preacher's signature," yet so many aspects of our preaching show the conscious and unconscious influence of our models. Sometimes we may suffer from model muddle. Robert W. Dale always kept the writings of Edmund Burke within reach and his highly logical and very doctrinal preaching bears the proof. John Henry Jowett is considered "the stylist of the English pulpit," and perhaps no one of this century has used the English language more beautifully in preaching. James Stewart of Scotland, personally very reserved in manner, had "a richly begemmed and enameled style." Thomas Chalmers caught fire slowly and Henry Van Dyke could strut while sitting down. Benjamin Franklin was an avid student of Joseph Addison and Richard Steele's *Spectator* essays and they greatly colored his style. It is said that Francis Patton quoted from Tennyson's "In Memoriam" at least once in every sermon he preached.

Preaching is a highly personal process; hence there is no such thing as the model or perfect sermon. We all wrestle with what Clyde Fant calls "the painful embarrassment of preaching—putting God's truth in human form." That someone has counted 2,930 different biblical personalities testifies to God's use of diversity and individuality. Ralph Waldo Emerson warns that, while we must study the masters, we must take ourselves as our portion. As those prone to imitate, we sometimes take on the idiosyncratic characteristics of our heroes. My own life was so greatly enriched by the variegated styles of the preachers I heard in my boyhood in the Twin Cities— Gustaf F. Johnson, William Bell Riley, Earle V. Pierce, George Vallentyne, Paul S. Rees, and Billy Graham during his early years in Minneapolis. We all live in a debt which will never be retired. It is profitable for all of us to analyze how and at what points our models have positively and negatively influenced us.

Michelangelo worked with a candle on his forehead in order to keep his own shadow off the surface. Our shadow will unavoidably fall on our work. There is a kind of originality and "cuteness" in preaching which really stems from arrogance and egotism. This is the peril of the pulpit idol or dilettante. P. T. Forsythe has a good word about "the pulpit prince," a caution we all need: "He is not in the pulpit, primarily, as the place where he can get the most scope for his own individuality, and most freedom for his own idiosyncrasy. He is there, both as the servant of the Word and the Church, to do a certain work, to declare a certain message, to discharge a certain trust. . . . He is not in the pulpit as the roomiest place he has found to enable him to be himself, and to develop his genius."[1]

To be genuinely and authentically ourselves in the pulpit is to be original in the proper sense. It is often said that to borrow from one is plagiarism, but to borrow from one thousand is research. Just as the preacher doing exegesis can go too quickly to the commentaries and deprive himself of really rooting around in the text, so the preacher can go too soon to the written sermons of others and short-circuit his own homiletical travail. The problem of being original is compounded under the heavy pressure of time shortage. We must do our own work in our own way if we are to be truly blessed. Said Touchstone in *As You Like It:* "An ill-favored thing, sir, but mine own!" In using the materials of others, we should heed the guidelines which Al Fasol has developed: be inspired but do not copy; give credit where credit is due;

---

1. P. T. Forsyth, *Positive Preaching and the Modern Mind* (Chicago: Allenson, 1921), 70.

be especially conscious of using illustrative material with integrity.[2]

We must never mistake our own incompetence or laziness with the way of the cross. There are preachers who feel inadequate and are plagued with basic tool deficiencies. We are all inadequate if the truth were told. It is encouraging to read Martin Luther's reaction to his own first sermon: "Oh how I trembled when I was ascending the pulpit for the first time! I fain would have excused myself, but they made me preach!" The gifted Augustine was no less uncertain:

> My preaching almost always displeases me. For I am eager after something better, of which I often have an inward enjoyment before I set about expressing my thoughts in audible words. Then, when I have failed to utter my meaning as clearly as I conceived it, I am disappointed that my tongue is incapable of doing justice to that which is in my heart. The chief reason is that the conception lights up the mind in a kind of rapid flash; whereas the utterance is slow, lagging and far unlike what it would convey.[3]

And so it ever is with those who would preach.

I want to suggest some important stylistic characteristics all preachers should share, apart from our very personal stylistic touches.

We need to be biblical. Charles Haddon Spurgeon said of John Bunyan that "his blood was Bibline." Luther wanted above all to be captive to the Word of God. It is not our comments that provide the change agent, but the living and powerful Word of God. James I of England complained on occasion of the court preacher's work, "It is not preaching, it is playing with the text."

2. Al Fasol, "Preaching the Material of Others with Integrity," *Church Administration* 30, 2 (November 1987): 28–9.

3. Augustine, *De Catechizandis Rudibus,* chapter 2.

The paradox of preaching is profoundly, "I, but not I. . . ." It is that which is beyond ourselves from God himself and his Word that will leave footprints on the sands of time. Snack-bar sermons won't do it. Verbal prestidigitation won't do it. Lavender-water theology won't do it. Hearsay evidence isn't acceptable. The psychological interpretation of life supplies nothing to sustain morality or true community. The "Lord, have you read the New York *Times?*" approach won't carry it. "Preach the Word," enjoins the apostle Paul in 2 Timothy 4:2.

Such biblicality in preaching is hard work, but as Sir Joshua Reynolds in his memorable *Lectures on Painting* comments, "God does not give excellence to men, but as the reward of labor." When we stop studying, we stop. What is true of seminarians is true of preachers everywhere: You can bring a student to seminary, but you can't make him think. Ads offering earned doctorates for nonresidents in nine to twelve months indicate how appealing brainless short cuts are and how happy we can all be in avoiding hard work and toil.

When the moderator of the Church of Scotland shares in the coronation of British royalty, he gives the new king or queen a Bible and says: "The most precious thing this world affords, the most precious thing that this world knows, God's living Word." This is the treasure we have to share and it is our awesome duty not to decide what it means but to discover what it means. Saint Bernard preached a series of eighty-five sermons on the first two chapters of the Song of Solomon. John Howe in seventeenth-century England preached fourteen sermons on the expression in Romans 8:24, "We are saved by hope," and seventeen sermons on 1 John 4:20 and eighteen sermons on John 3:6. If homiletics literally means "to say the same thing as" what the text says, even such fine-lined attention to the sacred text requires our asking of God and ourselves, "Is this truly biblical?"

Sometimes our sovereign God will use an infinitesimal

part of the text to touch some needy heart, or even to save a man who testifies that he came to Christ as the result of the preacher saying, "We move now from the first part to the second part." The man under conviction was compelled to think: "Well, you have to finish the first part of your life and start a second part." This is the amazing power of the Word of God through the Spirit. When the celebrated freethinker, Charles Bradlaugh, challenged Hugh Price Hughes to debate, the latter accepted on the condition that each bring one hundred persons whose lives had been changed by his respective teaching. Bradlaugh never showed up, and the one hundred whom Hughes brought turned the great assemblage into a testimony meeting.

James M. Wall observes that the environment of ministry today "is increasingly geared to surface appearances. The mass media—television, newspapers, magazines—and the culture they shape reward the superficial, the facile, the predictable. Preaching in such an environment is like rowing upstream. Occasionally it is tempting to rest the oars and float with the current. But these few restful moments result in the boat's drifting even further downstream."[4] In such a setting, the need for a style of biblical preaching is all the more urgent. Robert Murray McCheyne had the right perspective: "We have an inch of time in which to stand and preach Christ, then the endless roll of eternal years."

We need to be faithful. "Be prepared in season and out of season" (2 Tim. 4:2) is a timely call to a steady and sturdy ministry of the Word. In a very real sense preaching is the art of making a preacher, amassing a great soul and then delivering it. The sermon is the preacher up to date. We're really talking about an aspect of character here, and character is fidelity to God's vocation. Every season in ministry poses its peculiar temptation

4. James M. Wall, "Facing Reality in a Superficial Culture," *Christian Century* 101 (February 1–8, 1984), 99.

to swerve and deviate from the course set before us.
Early on the minister must revise expectations to meet
the realities of the work; the danger is to have high
enough expectations in the middle years in ministry and
courage when finally coming down the stretch. It is our
task to make the gospel available, not to make it acceptable, yet it is easy for us to become discouraged. Adver-
sities can soften us or harden us. When Jonathan
Edwards was asked to leave Northampton, Massachu-
setts, after twenty-four eventful years, he left without
bitterness or rancor. He kept climbing.

The frailty of the clay jug appalls us all. D. L. Moody
so murdered the king's English that he always pro-
nounced Nebuchadnezzar as one syllable; Spurgeon and
Matthew Simpson were severe melancholics; A. T. Robertson had a hesitation in his speech; neither Phillips
Brooks nor George Morrison had carrying voices; John
Henry Jowett had pernicious anemia and was always
frail; Richard Sibbes stammered; Ernest Manning
sniffed and snorted. This is not so different from any
other field of accomplishment. William Wordsworth was
hideously ugly but who thinks of it? Josiah Wedgewood
was an invalid, and John Dryden's nephew said to him:
"you will never be a poet." So G. Campbell Morgan was
turned down for the ministry in his first examination.
Scotsman James Macgregor had such deformed limbs he
despaired of ministry, but God gave him forty magnificent years at Saint Cuthbert's in Edinburgh. Henry P.
Liddon was so beneath the weight of his human weakness that he wrote on the night before he began his ministry at Saint Paul's in London that he felt very unequal
to the task, physically and emotionally. Who is sufficient
for these things? Only God makes us able ministers of
the new covenant. When David Livingstone was to
preach his first student sermon at Standford Rivers in
Scotland he completely blanked out. Later he wrote, "I
am still a very poor preacher and have bad delivery; and

some say that if they knew I was to preach, they would not enter the chapel." It is important that we learn to fail successfully. Lincoln was defeated seven times in political elections. Benjamin Disraeli failed at everything he tried in journalism and writing. Babe Ruth struck out more times than anyone else in baseball. But they kept on.

Two enemies can undermine faithfulness. On the one hand flattery, the professional aphrodisiac, can create a craving for applause. On the other hand we can become intoxicated with the fumes of modesty to believe that we are without value and can do nothing. The prophet Daniel's durability in the sixth century B.C. Peyton Place in which he lived bears ample testimony to God's sustaining and keeping power. He is faithful and he calls us to be faithful to death.

We need to be zestful. While we need dignity and not pomposity in the pulpit we have got to show a little zip and energy in the proclamation. How can we conceivably seem to be blasé about holy things? A traveler on a dark night met a man who hesitantly suggested, "I think there is some question on the bridge ahead . . . I think I heard something to the effect that there is a problem . . . It may be you should pause and reconsider." But the traveler went on. Then along came another man, rushing breathlessly, who confronted the traveler: "Stop! Go no farther! The bridge is out!" This message convinced and compelled. John Brown of Haddington in Scotland was said to have spoken of God with such fervor that the skeptic David Hume commented that "he preaches as if Jesus Christ were at his elbows." Each of us must find his or her own rhythms but the music needs to complement the words in preaching. Learning to vary sentence length and limiting the number of subordinate clauses can get us moving more vigorously in discourse. We need to consciously reflect on our style and seek to do something remedial about it.

Occasionally a student or a preacher will respond that his speaking pattern reflects who he is, and it would be an affectation to be something different. Of course this is nonsense; education has as its objective the implementation of change. Improvement and development of skills are mandatory. Even a preacher who is reserved can foster greater assertiveness and confidence. I offer a course at the divinity school on impromptu speaking. This course is not a preparation for the pulpit but provides opportunity and exercise for some creative self-talk. I have also found that a little book by Randolph Sanders and H. Newton Maloney is a most useful tool to build confidence.[5] Some preachers are severely hampered by shyness in speaking, but they are not alone. Forty percent of the general population testify that anxiety regarding public speaking is their most dominating fear. There is help for shy people and a shy preacher has a big challenge.[6]

We need to be relational. An effective preaching style explores the depths of "I–thou" intimacy between speaker and listeners. The preacher needs to be audience-conscious and people-sensitive, suffusing what he says with warm vibes and fuzzies. Of one preacher it was said that there was no core to his conversation—he was like a gramophone record; the person was absent. A president of Dartmouth College was criticized for his impersonal style. He was talking to his daughter about the matter and inquired, "Susan, do you think I'm cold, aloof, and noncommunicative?" Her reply said much: "Oh no, Mr. President, I don't think so." Could that be an impression of our preaching?

Textbook proficiency is not the issue here. The student of botany who can reel off information and descriptions but who cannot identify an actual flower has parallel in

5. Randolph K. Sanders and H. Newton Maloney, *Speak Up: Christian Assertiveness* (Philadelphia: Westminster, 1985).
6. Vincent Bozzi, "Serious Shyness," *Psychology Today* 19 (July 1985): 12.

ministry. Living in the time between advents as we do, we face people who have been privatized, pulverized, and polarized. We may not always cure but we can always care. The character Biff in *Death of a Salesman* plaintively says, "I just can't take hold, Mom, I just can't take hold of some kind of life." Edna St. Vincent Millay despairs, "Life must go on, I just forgot why." By the year 2000, if the Lord tarries, 50 percent of the children in our country will be raised in single-parent homes. Our preaching style needs to be warmly personal and the preacher needs to be approachable and accessible.

We need to be clear. James W. Cox reports that Spurgeon occasionally felt that his style was becoming too smooth. He then would read Thomas Carlyle, whose more angular style helped him to put more life into his preaching.[7] How seriously do we reflect on such nuances in our preaching? Is our discourse thickening and becoming opaque?

In a desire to become profound, we sometimes become polysyllabic. Our great desire ought to be to make our ideas clear. This is the great value of writing on a regular basis. If we can write clearly we shall be able to speak clearly. Sometimes when we experience the greatest difficulty in preaching we may be hard to understand because we use the language of Zion but do not explain or interpret it. The abandonment of basic biblical terminology such as "justification by faith" is not advisable, but it is certainly necessary to translate such terms into an understandable frame of reference. The concept of "accepting the unacceptable" is very close and much clearer.

We need to be real. Phoniness is not easy to judge at first, but what is genuine will show itself within the innumerable contexts of interaction. For example, the pastor may talk aplenty about caring for people, then

7. James W. Cox, *Preaching* (San Francisco: Harper and Row, 1985), 224.

bring that concern into question when a baby's cry intrudes into the sermon with an intensity only slightly lower than the sound of a pneumatic jackhammer. How the preacher reacts to such an interruption describes how he really views the value of another person. The enemies of Demosthenes attempted to prevent his obtaining leadership by appealing for an examination of the reality of his life, "not what he professes to be, but what he is: redoubtable in words, impatient in deeds; plausible in speech, perfidious in action." If we want the church to be a radiant bride and not a nagging wife, we must set an example in tone and texture. We have been told not to worry about what people are thinking of us because they aren't. But congregations do think about their pastor. Is something "real" coming through?

Catherine Drinker Bowen's biography of the brilliant Sir Francis Bacon describes how he was convicted of taking bribes while in high office and then was disgraced and banished from London. She records one of his prayers as he reflects on the squandering of his life as the result of losing the inner battle to "the evil that ambushes from within." As he writes: "So as I may truly say, my soul hath been a stranger in the course of my pilgrimage."[8] A consistent, deeply dependent, truly humble spirit of seeking after God is paramount.

These are generic characteristics of style which I covet and for which I pray. The rest will tend to be right within the glorious diversity of the Lord's endowment and enduement if these thrive and flourish by his grace. Marcus Dods, the scholar and writer, said in the dusk of the nineteenth century that he did not envy those who would carry the banner of Christianity into the twentieth century. Then he mused, "Yes, perhaps I do, but it will be a stiff fight." The battle is rough and the stakes are high. Concern for style in preaching should not be technolotry,

8. Quoted in Gordon MacDonald, *Restoring Your Spiritual Passion* (Nashville: Oliver-Nelson, 1986), 107.

the worship of method and technique, but the valid concern of how our own personalities come through and influence our preaching.

In the cathedral in Dijon, France, by no means an architecturally distinguished edifice, there sits over against the pulpit an angel with a pen. The angel tilts toward the pulpit as if expectant. People, angels, and God listen and evaluate. Karl Barth was a strong believer in preaching. "On Sunday morning when the bells ring to call the congregation and minister to church, there is in the air an expectancy that something great, crucial, and even momentous is to happen," he said.[9] Will such be the case? Is there such a sense among us? It seems almost too much for frail creatures such as we are to even contemplate. Augustus Saint Gauden's famous statue of Phillips Brooks in Boston gives us a good focus on what is involved: Brooks's left hand is on the Bible and his right hand gestures as he preaches. Behind him is the Lord Jesus Christ with his fingers on the preacher's left shoulder. It is reported that the sculptor, after reading the life of Brooks, asked for the Gospels and was converted in reading them. Our sufficiency is of God.

9. Karl Barth, *The Word of God and the Word of Man,* Trans. Douglas Horton (New York: Harper and Row, 1957).

15

How Can We Enhance the Presentation?
The Issue of Delivery

"**I**f you bore the jury, you have lost the case," insists a top liability lawyer. Preaching has been called the finest of the arts. The preaching art involves skill in design (the private aspect) and skill in delivery (the public aspect). Skills in delivery do not receive significant attention in many books on preaching or in many curricula for the training of preachers, yet we can lose it all here. Who can deny the critical importance of the oral transmission of the ideas to every aspect of the process?

There must, we again stress, be substantive ideas to communicate. All of our efforts to finesse delivery will be in vain if there is not fruitful study. Said an old brother to a preacher: "If I were a fox I would hide in the place you would never find me." "And where might that be?" queried the preacher. "In your study," was the reply.

The sense of fresh discovery is equally important. An elderly doctor boasted that he had practiced medicine for forty years. "No," his colleague thought, "in reality you have practiced one year forty times." Is it so with us?

Delivery must basically come from our own natures. Dr. Virgil Anderson of Stanford University said there is no one right way to do it, but there are many less effective ways we may try to do it. Some will be conversational and some oratorical, but no one can preach in a one-on-one style. When, as Peter, we raise our voice and address the crowd (Acts 2:14), we are in a different mode of communication.

God's servants are to be "flames of fire" (Heb. 1:7); preaching does need some thunder and lightning if people are to listen amid the clatter and competition of conflicting voices. The desire to communicate the truth instead of just to state the truth must be an obsessive compulsion. Meticulous research impregnated with prayer needs to be combined with some "show-biz" instincts. I'm unabashed to insist that increasingly this is what it takes. Jesus used drama and so must we. I'm not advocating a bubblebath of perpetual emotion, but I am saying we cannot be colorless, hesitating nonentities in dittoland. I would rather have to cool off a fanatic than warm up a corpse in preaching lab.

Thomas Guthrie was right when he said that in preaching "the manner is to the matter like gun-powder is to the ball." We need to be into it as we preach, responding to what we say as we are saying it. The preacher with congenital emotional languor shrinks back at this juncture. Our aim here is to imbue such preachers with what Frederick W. Robertson of Brighton, England, called "the intense excitement of preaching." If our preaching is like swimming in molasses, there are remedial steps to be taken. If our hearers listen like a lump of dough, it may be our fault. If our sermons seem to fizzle out like wet firecrackers, we've got some homework to do.

No practitioner of the craft can afford to rust on his laurels. If, in telling stories, we do poorly what the Bible does well, we need to get to work. Are we determined to dazzle? Do we tend to explain too much? We need to work on being not too subtle but direct.

Frequently on Saturday morning about eleven o'clock I would go into the sanctuary at First Covenant Church in Minneapolis, sit in my pulpit chair, and preach through my morning message for the next day. I would preach to the galleries and to specific individuals on the Chicago Avenue side and then to my left on the lower level. The specificity of the faces and the needs of the people always moved me and prepared me to preach with more heart on the Lord's Day. I recommend such a practice as part of meaningful preparation.

Relaxation Is Requisite

James W. Cox asserts that the effective preacher is not so much formed as freed up. High levels of tension hinder communication, yet the preacher needs to be primed and just bursting with the truth of the Word. There need to be moments of effective intensity through the message, but the hypertense individual does not relate maximally with others. We are conscious of the tension. We need help in reducing self-consciousness. The apostle Paul was encouraged: "Be not afraid, but speak . . ." (Acts 18:9 KJV). A little trepidation and stage fright are good for us. We should not hope to be rid of the butterflies in our tummy but rather seek to make them fly in formation. The overly faint and nervous heart will elicit first pity and sympathy, then impatience.

High tension levels conspire against good, diaphragmatic breathing. Every preacher should master and review the miraculous physiology of speech with the help of a good basic speech text. When we are tense we breathe out rather than up. Belly breathing results in shortness of breath and choppy projection. The normal speaking voice should be able to project satisfactorily for four or five hours, but tension makes the voice taut and hoarse. Tension also causes a dry mouth. Every speaker should be well watered with room-temperature water, not ice water which constricts the vocal folds. A good lozenge for a scratchy throat (such as the Swedish product lakerol) is ideal without producing too much froth at the mouth as a side effect.

Some relaxation technique is important for the preacher. Without camera memory or eidetic imagery, memorized materials, force-fed at the last minute, are virtually impossible to recall. Memorization is best done in small doses over time with the aid of mnemonic devices. Before preaching, the communicator should do some upper-torso exercise and facial massage in order to facilitate positive and warm facial gesture. Let your jaw hang free—you may look like a true simian in the process, but this will help you loosen up.

Some preachers come across as "breathing out threatenings and slaughter." Some indeed may be angry persons but most are just uptight so that they seem to have a feistier-than-thou attitude. We are advocating not vehemency but vitality in preaching. Spontaneity or free expression of emotion require relaxation. Today's preaching must see the human being as a medley which includes feeling. Let those who mock feeling read Archibald MacLeish, distinguished poet and former Librarian of Congress:

> To feel emotion is at least to feel. The crime against life, the worst of all crimes is not to feel. And there was never, perhaps, a civilization in which that crime, the crime of torpor, of lethargy, of apathy, the snake-like sin of coldness-at-heart, was commoner than in our technological civilization in which the emotionless emotions of adolescent boys are mass produced on television screens to do our feeling for us, and a woman's longing for her life is twisted, by singing commercials, into a new detergent, family size, which will keep her hands as innocent as though she had never lived. It is the modern painless death, this commercialized atrophy of the heart. None of us is safe from it.

Yet biblical faith is the greatest soil out of which such
expression can grow, for as G. K. Chesterton so master-
fully said: "Nothing sublimely artistic has ever arisen out
of mere art . . . there must always be a rich moral soil
for any great aesthetic growth."

Reading the Scripture Aloud

A continuing challenge for the preacher is the public
reading of Holy Scripture. I am appalled that we who
trumpet our high view of the Scripture read it so poorly
in public. "Devote yourself to the public reading of Scripture," Paul admonishes Timothy (1 Tim. 4:13). With the
laity involved in more and more public reading, it is
imperative that pastors model careful public reading of
the Word of God. It is axiomatic that if we cannot read
well aloud, we shall not preach well.[1] All reading of Scripture is an interpretation. It requires the most careful
preparation. Do we think we can read just any passage
at the drop of a hat without study and preparation? One
of my colleagues and I teach a course in how to read
Scripture aloud. Each of us has a different style, but we
are committed to the proposition that the Word of God
deserves painstaking oral interpretation. As in preaching
itself, there should be considerable and appropriate variation in pace, pitch, volume, and punch.

Very few words and varied words should be used to
introduce the reading. Ample opportunity should be
given to the congregation to find the reading. Except
where a large pulpit Bible makes it impractical, I favor
holding the Scripture in hand during the reading to
afford more opportunity for vital eye contact. The very
manner in which the Word is handled and held conveys
a message. A more athletic pronunciation of words and

---

1. A marvelous new resource is Charles L. Bartow, *Effective Speech Communication in Leading Worship* (Nashville: Abingdon, 1988).

the massaging of certain sounds will help people grasp the interpretation.

This all takes more work and application, but these are nonnegotiables. Almost every profession demands continuing education. Should pastors and ministers do less? We need to keep honing our skills and not be satisfied with our levels of competence. Can we fairly say that the way we perform is adequate for the high calling we have received? If we professional talkers would learn to listen we would realize that interesting and stimulating things are happening, and we need to be a part of such growth. The speaking voice ought to be the lifelong project of every preacher. It is a critical tool to take good care of and use to maximum efficiency.

The Case for Preaching Without Notes

Historically, different methods have been employed in the delivery of the message. Charles G. Finney used the impromptu method early in his evangelistic itinerations but less so after he became pastor at Broadway Tabernacle in New York City and president of Oberlin. This is totally unacceptable today in any settled ministry, although one suspects its use is more widespread than one would care to admit. Surely in preparing preaching, as in planning worship, the Holy Spirit can lead us in anticipation of the event as surely as in the existential moment.

The reading of the sermon manuscript actually originated during the reign of King Henry VIII of England. This is the most difficult and the least acceptable of the methods used in our day. The great problem with it is that it sounds written and read. The visual society in which we live has plunged us into a new communications ball game. The world of print must yield to the speech event, and television viewers are accustomed to communicators who do not rely on written materials. Only occasionally are we aware of cue cards. New and sophisticated technology enables the president to deliver his State of the Union address without any apparent reference to written data.

But long before television it was realized that reading the sermon creates distance. Herbert H. Farmer convincingly argued that the direct encounter with the will is hampered when the sermon is read. Paper is not a good conductor of heat. The complaint was registered of a preacher that he read his sermon; he didn't read it well; and it wasn't worth reading. Certainly the prevailing practice is to reduce prepared materials to small notes to be taken into the pulpit. Long, read quotations and passages are poor form, although occasional reference to notes is reassuring to many preachers, especially as they start out. Every break in eye contact is risky, especially when that break comes toward the end of the sentence and is often accompanied by voice-drop. The late Bishop Fulton J. Sheen abandoned all notes and written materials in his most effective presentations after hearing an elderly Irish lady complain, "If the father can't remember his own sermon, how can he expect us to remember it?"

The memorization of the entire sermon (*memoriter*) is not often attempted, although there have been those in the history of preaching who have used the method. Although eye contact is maintained memorization still uses the manuscript and has a decidedly written sound to it. The task is prodigious, and the result in most cases is still quite unsatisfactory.

The extempore or free-delivery method is best suited to today's preaching situation and is well worth serious consideration. If freedom is the rule in front of an audience, this method is preferred. Harry Emerson Fosdick began to read his sermons and felt nothing was sacrificed, but a serious study has concluded that he was not as effective in communication after he forsook free delivery. Congregational feedback indicated to one young preacher that leaving his dependence on a manuscript, improving eye contact and gestures, and becoming more relaxed had greatly improved his preaching effectiveness. The eye is really an organ of speech. Indeterminate eye focus or too furtive an eye sweep is unsatisfying to listeners. Samuel Taylor Coleridge's famous line, "He holds him with his glittering eye" says it well. In any given congregation there are several faces which mirror response in a particularly helpful way. One must not look too much at any one, but it is better to look at six listeners than a dozen, for then eye contact becomes more than a quick glance.

In the British House of Commons, a member's speech may be cut short should someone say, "May I call attention to the fact that the honorable member is reading his remarks." George Whitefield was one of the first to preach without notes and was followed by many, including Charles Haddon Spurgeon, John Hall, Henry Ward Beecher, T. De Witt Talmadge. Richard Storrs gave us an early volume advocating free delivery after he noted that a good lawyer never used notes in addressing his appeal to the jury.

Both Clarence Macartney and Charles Koller have given strong cases for preaching without notes, the latter arguing that this method is 40 percent preparation, 50 percent saturation, and 10 percent memorization. Free style requires clear and strong structure, growing vocabulary, and the hard work of deep saturation. I usually memorize my introduction, rivet the statement of the main points and transitions in and out of my illustrations and my closing sentences. Then I steep my mind and soul in the flow, preach certain sections aloud, and think paragraphically. If I can't get it into my head, it is likely my development is not coherent.

Preaching without notes or with minimal notes should be our goal, given the contemporary situation in communication. Certainly it is hard work, but few who try it ever leave the method. Ben Hogan practiced six to eight hours a day on his golf game. Albert Schweitzer would practice the musical intricacies of Bach's compositions the whole night long. If we are motivated to put more effort into oral communication we shall begin to see a new effectiveness in the pulpit.

Working with the Voice

Faith is an acoustical affair, as Romans 10:14 might be paraphrased to remind us. Notwithstanding the cult of the nonverbal, the spoken word is the primary form for language. "Watch your language" was always one of the chief pieces of advice Joseph Sittler gave to preachers. We need to be students of language, careful with grammar and syntax and masters of the English usage.

But all of this will be futile if we can't really be heard. Our speaking voice can get in the way. Some preachers are endowed with vocal registers of such quality and resonance as to elicit envy from the brethren. Such organ or violin-like tonality contrasts sharply with the dowdy drone. Some voices boom like a pack of hounds in full cry while others have the sound of mush. Whitefield had more than a gurgling obligato. Here was "preaching that startled a nation" and could on occasion be heard a mile away. Spurgeon warned against the pulpit whine, "sepulchral tones which may fit a man to be an undertaker but Lazarus is not called out of his grave by hollow moans." None of us should assume that the voice we have and our skills with it are enough for communication. The speaking voice can be developed within certain parameters. The urgency of our message should motivate us to seek improvement.

All preachers should have some voice analysis. Have we developed some inflective patterns which are obnoxious? Have we some screamer's nodes? Are we showing signs of voice strain? I have to personally work on voice drop. There are soft-palate exercises (with "da-da, ga-ga, la-la" sounds) which build the musculature of the lower registers and enhance timbre and resonance.

The apostle Paul apparently lacked a rotund voice, so let us be encouraged not just to make do but to work on our problems. Certainly we need to excise slang and minced oaths, which are most unbecoming from the pulpit. Sometimes our problem is lazy lips. We need to work on timing, rhythm, and specific sounds. Our goal is a well-modulated voice that lays the stress on the thought words, vowel duration, and inflection. For example, to pronounce Welsh words we are told we need a cold in the head, a knot in the tongue, and a husk of barley in the throat. We need to be aware of what makes sound (phonation), what shapes sound (articulation), and what amplifies sound (resonation). It is better to speak a little faster than average (up to 190 words per minute) than too slowly because this is heard as enthusiasm and passion. Phillips Brooks was virtually inaudible the first time he spoke in Westminster Abbey. He took one hundred voice lessons and no complaints were heard when he spoke there again.[2] Would it not be worth it for the preacher to give some serious consideration to the voice by which the message of life and death will be proclaimed?

The Significance of the Nonvocal

Cicero had eloquence in his fingertips and of the English actor David Garrick it was said that "by moving his elbow he could produce an effect no words could achieve." Grooming and posture make a statement before one even begins to speak. It is important in body language that the words and music go together. The human

2. Ralph M. Harper, "Phillips Brooks' Voice Lessons," *Church Management* 24 (January 1947).

face can make five hundred thousand different expressions. Today, with facial hair popular, we have to deal with preachers who obscure positive facial gestures or the smile.

David Lloyd-George advised against use of the hands or wrists but counseled that only the arms be used in gesture. Only gestures from the shoulder say very much; small, blurred gestures convey only intensity. Useful gestures are descriptive, emphatic, or directive. Anything we do often or habitually is not very effective. Thus the praying-mantis gesture, the ring twist, or the wood chop become nervous gestures which distract. Every preacher should be videotaped every few years for a critique of form and silly habits that can obtrude. I recall a professor who helped me greatly by pointing out that I launched the sermon with an elevation of my nostrils like a bull pawing the ground. It was a gesture of arrogance and needed prompt attention.

Henry Wadsworth Longfellow picked up something from one preacher: "I could not tell what he was driving at, except that he seemed desirous not to offend the congregation." Our manner communicates. Abraham Lincoln said he loved to hear a preacher who spoke as if fighting a swarm of bees. He remembered a preacher who had to have two bricks in his pockets to keep him in his place. Movement, of course, should be meaningful, and pulpit wandering is just another kind of blurred gesture. Some preachers thrash like fish in shallow water. There seems to be a rather tigerlike tendency in the preacher who paces back and forth. Henry Venn impressed his auditors as looking like he was about to jump out of the pulpit. It has become stylish in some circles to disregard the pulpit in preaching. I think it is best to start in the pulpit at least. In some of our more low-church settings, the pulpit may be one of the few Christian symbols in the room. To move meaningfully away or to draw nearer in a gesture of intimacy can be positive. Hands in the pocket or behind the back are gestures of nonchalance or distance and do us no good. The chin wag or the head toss are read negatively pretty well across cultural lines. Studies have shown how facial expressions affect listeners even physiologically.[3]

Is there any challenge greater than that which comes to the gospel communicator as we face down the stretch of this century? Across the whole vast waterfront of matters relating to delivery, we must pray with Thomas More: "The good things, good Lord, that we pray for, give us the grace to labor for."

---

3. Jeff Meer, "Reagan's Facial Teflon," *Psychology Today* 20 (January 1986): 18.

Index of Subjects

Index of Scripture

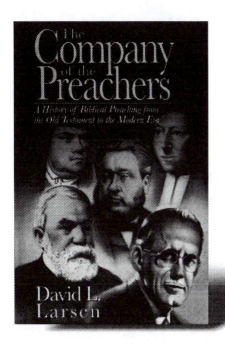

The Company of the Preachers
by David L. Larsen

0-8254-3128-x, 894 pages

This comprehensive work by a seasoned pastor and professor of homiletics provides an extensive look at the history of preaching from its roots in the Old Testament prophets to its continuing development in the modern era. Pastors, Bible college and seminary students, and all who enjoy history will appreciate the information and insights in this valuable reference resource.

> "A work like this has been needed for some time and it is with enthusiasm that I commend this monumental work on the history of preaching."
>
> —Walter C. Kaiser Jr.

> "This work will inspire all of us to reaffirm our unique high calling of preaching God's Word. It will also give us fresh input on how to improve our preaching by gaining insights from the great communicators of the past."
>
> —Erwin W. Lutzer

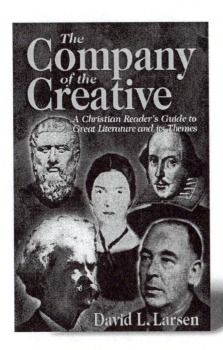

The Company of the Creative
by David L. Larsen

0-8254-3097-6, 656 pages

Many pastors and laypeople with minimal liberal arts background are interested in reading and analyzing the classics of literature but don't know where to start. Here is a study of the great works and authors of world literature from a Christian perspective. Each work is introduced and described and then reviewed artistically, intellectually, and theologically.

Periods and genres examined are the Classics, the Renaissance and Reformation, epic poetry, British poetry, American fiction, African and Latin American literature, Jewish literature, essays, and biographies. Authors discussed include Plato, John Milton, Charles Dickens, William Shakespeare, Charlotte Brontë, and C. S. Lewis.

A great resource for sermon illustrations!